Praise for *Why Good Is Hard*

I'll be honest with you—this book hit close to home. As someone who leads both an environmental incubator and an organization centered on the virtues that make us better humans, I've sat with that quiet frustration Tim describes: Why is doing the right thing so hard?

Tim doesn't sugarcoat it. From the opening pages, he lays out what he calls the "Six Horsemen of Difficulty"—and spoiler alert, altruism isn't one of our primary motivators. But here's the gift: once you stop expecting goodness to sell itself, you can actually get to work.

This book is, at its core, a masterclass in marketing. Understanding your audience, crafting your value proposition, building community, telling compelling stories—Tim walks through each of these with real research and real examples. If you're leading a purpose-driven company or nonprofit, this is your playbook. Not because it tells you what's right, but because it shows you how to make people want what's right.

The book is also a quiet call to perseverance. Change is hard. Resistance is real—from competitors, from culture, from the very people you're trying to help. Tim reminds us that steadfastness isn't naive; it's strategic. You have to stay in the arena long enough to build trust, shift habits, and move hearts.

—Dave Feldman,
Executive Director, Bethesda Green

In *Why Good Is Hard,* Tim strips away the vanity metrics to reveal the actual mechanics of change. He challenges both non-profits and even commercial businesses to stop chasing visibility and start focusing on market adoption.

The centerpiece of this approach is Tim's Minimum Viable Product (MVP) framework. It demands a brutal assessment of pain points before you commit to a single campaign.

The "SUV Pivot" in the book is the gold standard for this logic. Most groups market their mission of "off-road capability" when the market is actually buying "safety and utility." If you miss that distinction, you miss the market.

Social impact groups often mistake noise for influence. They get lost in the cause and forget to deliver a functional solution. This book provides the detailed framework needed to stop the "feel-good" drift and actually plan for the future.

Mission statements are just paper. Real leadership is proven by the integrity of your outreach.

When you ignore acute, local pain points, you've already failed the market and entering a slow, expensive slide into the status quo.

Tim Young offers the structural fix. He ensures your positioning is a sincere representation of your group, that is built specifically for the people who actually need the solution.

—Jonathan Graham,
Past Chair, Sustainable Green Printing Partnership

WHY GOOD IS HARD

WHY GOOD IS HARD

BREAKTHROUGH MESSAGING STRATEGIES FOR SOCIAL AND ECONOMIC CHANGE

TIM YOUNG

Precocity Press

Copy Editor: Emerald Gao
Creative Director: Susan Shankin
Cover Design: Sonia Horne
Book Design and Layout: Andrea Reider
Charts and Graphs: Tim Kummerow
Precocity Press, Los Angeles, CA

ISBN: 978-1-972561-02-7 (Trade Paperback)
ISBN: 978-1-972561-03-4 (eBook)
Library of Congress Control Number: 2026908399
First edition printed in the United States of America

To my family, who are the reason I write.

Contents

Preface

If you've ever tried to make a positive change in the world, you've very likely felt despair. Those with resources seem only to care about their own enrichment. Those with the power to make change find that it's easier to pay lip service to a cause than take effective action. Common sense initiatives become untouchable political hot buttons, and we rarely see our enthusiasm for our mission reflected in our friends, neighbors, and colleagues.

At the end of a long day, when you haven't made nearly as much progress as you'd like, you've probably found yourself wondering if any shred of hope is worth keeping in a world that seems besieged by fear, anger, and greed.

You are not alone. This book is for you.

Millions of people all over the world are working to solve humanity's most pressing problems. We are chipping away at climate change, wealth inequality, exploitative capitalism, and political tension. We are doing it from within corporations, nonprofits, our communities, and our own homes. And while our solutions never seem to reach the same volume as the reactionary screaming on cable news and social media, getting a positive message heard and making a small measure of change in the world is possible. All we need to do is stop viewing that change through an idealistic lens, take off our gloves, and start slugging it out with our competitors.

It will not be a fair fight. But no one said it was going to be.

The purpose of this book is to help you, the would-be do-gooder, understand how the modern marketing and communications landscape functions so that you can gain public, commercial, and political attention—as well as tangible support—for your cause.

My goal is to give you a clear messaging model you can use to triumph over the naysayers, negative nellies, and your own doubts in order to deliver positive, sustainable change. The development process for a detailed communications strategy will ask you some tough questions about your goals, your preparation, and the steps you're willing to take in order to deliver your change. We've got some tough sledding ahead, but I know you're up for the challenge.

Because good is hard, but giving up is far, far worse.

1

Why Good is Hard

A few years ago, one of my clients in the printing business was trying to convince a large international food and beverage franchise to use recycled paper for its cups instead of virgin stock. Using recycled material would generate great publicity for the company, which was seeking an environmental public relations win to back up recent sustainability pledges, and the discussions felt promising. My client was even thinking that the deal would be featured in her customer's upcoming annual report. There was only one problem: each recycled cup would cost a few fractions of a penny more to produce.

When you're selling millions of cups a day, those fractions add up, and the deal unfortunately fell through after months of negotiations. Then, just a few weeks later, the chain announced that it would eliminate plastic straws. The press hailed the move as an environmental win, and conveniently glossed over the fact that the decision saved the franchise a few fractions of a cent on every cup.

My client was frustrated. She'd already spent long years and tens of thousands of dollars developing more sustainable business practices and products, only to run into a wall. Had she wasted all that time and effort? Why was traction on sustainable products so challenging when she was trying to do the right thing for the planet?

In other words, why was good so hard?

If you're trying to promote a positive cause, grow a sustainable product, build a more circular supply chain, or make some other worthy change in the world, you've likely asked yourself the same question. It could have come up after a long day of facing off with short-sighted politicians, intractable community members, or harried consumers who just don't seem to care. It could have come in a management presentation when finance shuts down your idea for being too costly. Or it could have come in a quiet moment when you wonder what the point of even trying is, when an international franchise can win praise for greenwashing while you worry about keeping your company in business.

The frustrations involved in creating positive change can be immense and demoralizing, but they do not have to defeat you. Through a combination of research and experience, this book will answer the question of "why good is hard." Armed with that knowledge, you'll uncover solutions that will give you a better chance of bringing your change to life and making a small positive dent in the universe.

Be warned: solving the problem will require a new way of thinking about, and promoting, your cause. We're going to dive deep into marketing strategy and product development theory to better position your cause to compete for your market's time and money, and that might mean making some hard choices about what you'll offer to your audience and how you'll deliver that change. It won't be easy, but if you do the work, you'll break through the barriers that cause marketers face.

So let's roll up our sleeves, set our feet, and figure out how to do some good.

THE SIX HORSEMEN OF DIFFICULTY

We're going to start by helping you understand the exact size of the mountain you're trying to climb. In the course of my research for this book, I uncovered six core reasons why good is hard:

1. **"Good" is not a primary human motivator.** Little evidence exists to show that human motivation is affected by qualities such as altruism. In fact, our minds are wired to respond to negative stimuli much more strongly than positive.
2. **Inertia resists change.** Existing economic systems and market conditions will always strongly resist change.
3. **We don't make people money.** Most "good" solutions tend to negatively impact revenue and profitability, which makes attracting investment and gaining economic traction challenging.
4. **Our value proposition isn't clear.** We struggle to clearly communicate why and how someone will directly benefit from supporting our cause.
5. **We're afraid to truly compete.** We compete for time and attention with better resourced, more entrenched companies operating from zero-sum mindsets, but few of us acknowledge that competition for our cause's survival.
6. **We lack power.** We focus on influencing those with the power to change, rather than taking that power for ourselves.

Together, these factors can help explain a concept known as the **value-action gap,** which simply means that people do not always act in accordance with their stated values. So while a company may claim to support the environment when considering the type of paper stock to use in its cups, in reality the company chooses its actions based on some combination of the factors above.

Let's examine each in detail.

"Good" Is Not a Motivator

What motivates a human being? Why do we get out of bed, brush our teeth, and join a cause? Philosophers, sociologists, and psychologists have spent lifetimes trying to answer these questions. Albert Einstein is quoted (likely apocryphally) as saying, "Three great forces rule the world: stupidity, fear, and greed." Market psychologists, perhaps a more cynical bunch, reduce those possibilities by 33 percent, eliminating stupidity. In their view, the only observable motivators are:

- **Fear:** we act when we are in danger of losing something
- **Greed:** we act when we can gain something

Despite all appearances, this isn't a cynical book, and the good news is that market psychologists aren't the only ones studying human behavior. Human motivation is by no means a settled science. We will continue to baffle each other in new and different ways on a daily basis (particularly in election years), and we will continue to develop new theories of motivation as a result. The commonly accepted theories tend to classify the sources of human motivation as some combination of the following:

- **Intrinsic needs** that slake our biology
- **Expectations** we seek to meet
- A **desire to achieve** or receive something (which could very likely be created by the first two items above)

The specifics will vary depending on which of the core motivational theories outlined below you subscribe to, but our deepest subconscious motivations appear to center around factors such as food, shelter, dopamine, and a handful of other inputs.[1]

Let's review a few theories in detail.

Evolutionary Theory

If you've ever heard of "survival of the fittest," you'll be familiar with evolutionary theory. The theory holds that humans' primary motivation is to improve their odds of survival and reproduction while expending the least amount of energy to do so. From the perspective of evolutionary theory, we are primarily resource-driven because humans evolved at a time when finding enough food and surviving the dangers of the wild was not guaranteed. And while our resource gathering today might look like building our bank account or buying a house, underneath those desires (and likely completely subconscious for most people) is the simple motivation of survival.

Maslow's Hierarchy of Needs

In some ways a continuation of evolutionary theory, psychologist Abraham Maslow argued that once we've met our basic physiological and safety needs, we will next look for social needs like love and esteem. If our social needs are met, we will then progress to "self-actualized" motivators such as creativity, problem solving, and other pursuits that help us improve ourselves or (crucially for the readers of this book) the world around us.

Drive Reduction Theory

Drive reduction theory holds that we are constantly responding to our body's drives (for food, sex, sleep, etc.) in order to return our body to homeostasis. All other motivations are secondary to, and in service of, these primary motivations. So, we might work hard at our job in order to seek a raise, which we believe would make us more attractive to the opposite sex, which might all be underpinned by our desire to reproduce and then go take a nap.

Arousal Theory

This theory is similar to drive reduction, but focuses more narrowly on the dopamine arousal that we experience when presented with the opportunity to accomplish something and receive a reward. Arousal theory posits that we fixate on the anticipation from novel experiences due to dopamine's effect as a mental pleasure-driver.

Incentive Theory

Incentive theory holds that humans act in response to extrinsic (coming from outside of the individual) or intrinsic (coming from within ourself) motivational factors. In this model, intrinsic tasks we enjoy provide the greatest motivation, especially when we receive external validation for them in the form of praise, money, or other socially valued factors.

Cognitive and Achievement Approaches

These theories state that humans are motivated by successful achievement, and that we constantly use various cognitive approaches to identify, explain, and close the gaps between our current status and our desired achievement. This approach gives rise to the term "cognitive dissonance," which occurs when we are forced to confront the gap between our beliefs, our actions, and our achievement (or lack thereof). Cognitive dissonance can be painful, especially in regards to our own value-action gaps, and so we are (often subconsciously) motivated to reduce its impact.

Expectancy Theory

This theory proposes that motivation is a combination of our expectation for the successful outcome of any action; the belief that the better we perform, the greater reward we will receive; and the value we place on the expected outcome of our efforts. The more confident we are that we will achieve an outcome that comes with a reward, the more likely we will be to act.

Do you notice anything missing from the motivational theories above? Did you see anything related to altruism, or the greater good? What about the environment, or sustainability, or better governance, or any of the thousands of causes and improvements we're struggling to actualize today?

Unfortunately, these qualities are absent, primarily because human motivation, as far as scientists can tell, appears to be largely selfish and internal. In fact, many philosophers, sociologists, and psychologists doubt that true altruism exists.[2]

While this may feel like bad news, it doesn't mean we can't train or encourage others to value our cause. It just means it will take work, which we'll cover in Chapter 3.

Change is Difficult

People rarely like change. In fact, the idea of change can be so difficult for people to accept that an entire discipline of "change management" has emerged to help organizations cope with internal and external stresses related to shifting the status quo. And your idea of change, dear reader, is likely going to be a cause of great stress to an existing system.

While personal or professional changes can be challenging enough, industry and market changes up the ante considerably. You can get a sense for just how hard change is from the grim success statistics for new products and businesses:

- Between one-third and one-half of all new products fail.[3]
- Approximately 50 percent of new businesses never survive to their fifth year.[4]

Why are the scales tipped against change? Because when trying to change a category (or market, or industry), you're going up against a deck stacked by two different actors: competitors, and the market itself.

Competitive Resistance

Remember my client who was trying to sell recycled cups? If you want to know how she responded, she dusted herself off and submitted the next proposal, and the next, and the next. Because in business, if you're not growing, you're shrinking. And the only thing that companies hate more than declining revenues is change. Change creates market uncertainty and incurs costs, both of which impact revenues.

As a result, any number of better-resourced incumbents are going to view your change efforts as an existential threat. Competitive resistance strengthens as a function of market consolidation. The US economy has been moving closer to an oligarchy over the past few decades, which means that a small handful of extremely resource-rich, highly efficient competitors dominate the majority of US industries. And these competitors will fight tooth and nail to maintain their position.

Here's what that looks like in practical terms for you, as related by a former colleague's experience in the consumer packaged-goods industry. My colleague spent close to a year developing a new dishwasher soap that included an antibacterial agent. The concept tested very well with consumers, and no one in the industry had a similar product on the market. The product concept passed every internal decision gate, moved into production, and worked its way through the company's distribution centers. She was incredibly excited, as it looked like she had a big hit on her hands.

The day before her product was to hit store shelves, her legal department received a "friendly" letter from one of her competitors letting her know that they intended to challenge her antibacterial product claim on the basis of an obscure FDA ruling from the early 1990s. After much legal review, my colleague's company had to make the difficult decision to scuttle the product and destroy millions of units that were already sitting in warehouses rather than spend a potentially even larger sum on legal fees.

My biggest takeaway from this story? The fact that her competitors had monitoring in distribution centers around the country, and were able to react in a matter of days to stop a potential threat to their market share.

That's the kind of change resistance you're going to face. Chapters 2 and 3 will provide some concrete steps to help overcome it.

Market Resistance

Resistance from competitors is expected and understandable. But resistance from your target market (which we'll define in Chapter 2) is another challenge entirely.

It can be extremely costly and challenging to even let your market know that you exist. And once you've spent all that time and money, your potential change agents may still be reluctant to try your solution or join your cause for any number of reasons. The time and effort to do so could be too great, or they could be unwilling to risk a new choice. They might not know anyone who's tried your solution, or they might not trust a new entrant into the market.

Breaking through this resistance will require you to navigate much of the motivational psychology that we explored this chapter. We'll tackle that challenge in Chapter 5.

We Don't Make People Money

There's a sad saying in the world of conservation that a tree only makes money when you cut it down. And in a world driven by economic considerations, it's imperative to understand that a significant percentage of people view the challenges and causes we are trying to solve as a problem of dollars and cents.

Consider the situation of a landowner being encouraged to conserve their forest. That person still has to pay taxes on their land. If they struggle to keep up with those taxes, they may choose to log the land and be paid for the timber. That timber will then be sold to a mill, which will turn it into any number of products that will be sold to distributors and manufacturers, who ultimately will make money from products ranging from toothpicks to furniture to sawdust cat litter.

With apologies to orchardists, none of that economic activity could take place if that tree wasn't cut down. And that money will be a powerful motivator to every individual in that supply chain.

Going back to the failed cup sale that began this chapter, keep in mind that another business supplied the cups to my client's targeted prospect, which means that someone else who better met that prospect's needs made money, and my client didn't. If that pattern were to continue, all of my client's time and effort spent building a green business and selling green products would result in failure, because they'd be out of business.

So your solution needs to be economically viable, because everyone needs to pay the bills. There's just one problem: eco-friendly product solutions are generally 75–85 percent more expensive than conventional offerings,[5] with research showing that "willingness to pay a premium" is the most significant driver of these green purchases.[6]

In other words, if someone can afford it, they might pay for your "good" solution. But that's a significant risk, as the following example shows.

The Prius: A Hit that Nearly Wasn't

Did you know that the Prius, the world's most successful hybrid vehicle, was a flop when it launched?[7] Toyota found that its initial target audience of passionate environmentalists looking to use less gas were unfortunately also the kind of people who rarely bought new cars. Even worse, they considered a car a wasteful purchase. And when the manufacturer went looking for another market, its research showed that wider audiences balked at the car's high cost compared to its size.[8]

The Prius, and the entire category of hybrid vehicles in general, was very close to dead in the water. That is, until Toyota's headquarters worked out a lower-margin arrangement with its dealers that allowed the car to be sold below a $20,000 price point and still be (slightly) profitable.

Price mattered to consumers, who wouldn't buy an expensive compact sedan. And profit mattered to the dealers tasked with selling to those consumers.

You might think that you won't face these issues. Maybe you're a nonprofit, or maybe you're promoting a cause. But nonprofits have expenses just like any other business. And volunteers can only contribute so much before they need to make sure they can pay their own bills. You're competing for time or money no matter what cause you're promoting or who you're targeting. And your audience is going to be evaluating the impact of your request on their available time and money.

We'll examine how to approach this issue in Chapter 3.

Our Value Proposition Isn't Clear

We've touched on humans' selfish decision-making, and we've addressed the fact that our solutions are often more expensive. So it should be no surprise that causes often struggle to explain why someone should take action and support them in the first place.

People and businesses make decisions on how they will spend their time or money based on their perception of what they will gain in exchange for their effort. This concept is known as your **value proposition.**

We'll discuss how to create your value proposition in Chapter 3. But for now, know that an entire scientific discipline has been built around understanding and influencing human purchase motivation, and that discipline has identified five core drivers:

1. Convenience
2. Cost
3. Quality
4. Performance
5. Attractiveness

At the risk of sounding like a broken record, do you notice anything missing on that list? Once again, concepts like sustainability, or equality, or diversity, or any number of other positive traits that you're likely trying to communicate if you're reading this book are nowhere to be seen.

Those omissions aren't because researchers haven't asked about them. In fact, dozens of studies have. And over and over again, these studies have found that purchasers weigh convenience and cost more heavily than any other factor.[9]

Purchase decisions appear to be inherently selfish. A consumer in the grocery store picks a product with nonrecyclable packaging because it's more affordable than a competing brand. Or a publicly owned business selling millions of cups a day can't reconcile the earned media value of moving to recycled cups with the hit to its profit.

You can disagree with the list above, but we're approaching 70 years of scientific work in this area, performed by people with very distinguished research careers at major universities, for companies that stand to make a large amount of money by getting their value propositions right. These organizations have become marketing experts, and it's important to understand that they are putting out compelling messaging that's been researched and tested for decades.

If you aren't speaking that same language to your market when promoting your cause, your odds of breaking through are slim. Let's take a look at an example:

A Tale of Compost and Dumpsters

A few years ago, I helped a composting startup build its positioning as it sought to make the leap from proof-of-concept installations to paying customers. The owner was targeting urban restaurants and food service suppliers, which are generally lower-margin businesses, and these businesses saw a composting service as an additional waste removal cost instead of a value driver.

To make sales, we had to dig deeper into the cost structures of the waste removal industry. Significantly, we found that most customers were charged per dumpster "pull" (each time the waste company emptied a receptacle). On top of that, the waste management companies locked customers into long-term contracts that automatically increased the cost per pull by certain percentages every year.

Do you know what would reduce the number of dumpster pulls for every food-related business out there? Composting.

And so, a value proposition that began as "composting is easy and the right thing to do for the planet" shifted to "our service can cut your waste removal costs by 40 percent or more, starting on day one."

Within two weeks after switching up the messaging, the first paying customer signed up.

We're Afraid to Truly Compete

No matter your solution, you will be introducing it to an attention battleground. Those of us working on large, complex challenges that will take long periods of time to solve (global warming, income inequality, and the like) can't solve these issues alone, and must rely on the sustained attention, effort, and contributions of a host of volunteers, partners, and politicians. Yet these audiences face constant demands on their time that can easily pull their attention away from our efforts, and competitors with much deeper pockets and more immediate needs who are vying for their attention.

If you work for a corporation, you will be competing dollar-for-dollar with larger, better-resourced competitors. If you operate a nonprofit, you will be vying for the scraps of time and money that donors, foundations, and the public have left over after their day jobs.

So the question you will have to answer is, are you committed enough to truly compete? And by compete, I mean shift the economic power balance toward your solution.

It's one thing to protest, sign petitions, and write letters to your representatives to generate awareness about an issue. It's quite another to found a business and dedicate your life to being the change you want to see.

This decision can be terrifying.

A few years ago, I was talking to an individual at a sustainability conference who was in charge of product line packaging at a well-known food company. Our conversation turned to recycling, and I asked him how his company was approaching the issue. To my surprise, he told me his main focus was trying to improve recycling adherence among consumers.

It took me a moment to collect my thoughts. Here I was, at an event devoted to reducing plastic waste, talking to someone who had the power to directly solve that issue at his company. And instead of doing so, he was shifting responsibility for the waste his company was generating to his customers.

He could have struck out on his own. He told me he'd gotten a sustainability certificate. There was nothing stopping him from developing his own packaging line and taking it to every industry connection he had.

Except, he had a student loan and a mortgage and a family to provide for. And he knew just how hard starting a business would be.

He's not alone. Your for-profit competitors will typically have larger budgets, more sophisticated tools, and a better understanding of how to operate in and extract revenue from your market. And they will spend somewhere around 73 times more on advertising than nonprofits.[10, 11]

But if you're truly committed to making a change, you can create opportunities if you're willing to pull out all the stops to achieve that vision and provide something of value to the market.

Recent research has documented a growing short-term thinking trend in U.S. companies.[12] These effects appear to have accelerated since the COVID-19 pandemic, with companies facing serious pressure to show growing revenues in an uneven economic situation having to turn to the dual levers of cutting quality and raising prices. This pressure, combined with the challenge of satisfying investors looking for returns for large-scale investments that take significant capital to build and run, has created a phenomenon known as "enshittification."[13, 14]

The way to combat this trend is with better alternatives. And you could be that alternative.

We Lack True Power

I once had a conversation with a leader at a well-known cause-driven nonprofit, and we found ourselves discussing the organization's approach to change. This group is funded by donations and grants from a number of foundations and individual donors, and my counterpart said something that struck me: "Entrepreneurs aren't going to solve the problem."

As an entrepreneur, I was surprised because we often see ourselves as problem solvers. So I asked her to clarify.

Her perspective was that she had to focus her efforts on politicians because they wrote the laws. And then she started lamenting about all the competing lobbying pressure from other organizations that she faced.

That conversation crystallized something about power and change in my mind. I was sitting across the table from someone whose salary was paid for by donations from successful businesspeople and corporations, who knew that she was up against larger, better-funded competition. This individual chose to believe that politicians, who rely on political donations to fund their campaigns, would ultimately do the right thing if they were presented with the right arguments and polling data.

In short, this group was trying to effect significant economic change using the few crumbs that the country's financial power players let fall from their plate. And the minute a more powerful backer chose a different association, or a different politician, all bets were off.

The organizations and politicians that are making the decisions in your community are doing so because of the influence applied on them. And if you are not influencing them, you have not yet achieved the power to do so.

We'll discuss how to achieve this power in Chapter 8.

WHAT ARE WE GOING TO DO ABOUT IT?

So far, we've learned that humans are primarily selfish decision-makers who hate change, and weigh price and profit more heavily than anything else. We've also realized that our causes are competing against millions of other organizations, all vying for the same attention and dollars in the marketplace of ideas, that won't hesitate to slit our throats to save theirs.

If you've gotten this far, you might be a bit discouraged about your prospects. I can't say I blame you, because, after all, good is hard.

But I don't want you discouraged. I want you angry.

I want you ready to beat the market and your competitors at their own game. I want you fired up to make your cause the best-selling product in your market. And I want you to use this book as your marketing guide.

To do so, we're going to follow the steps below, based on the product development and marketing decision funnels:

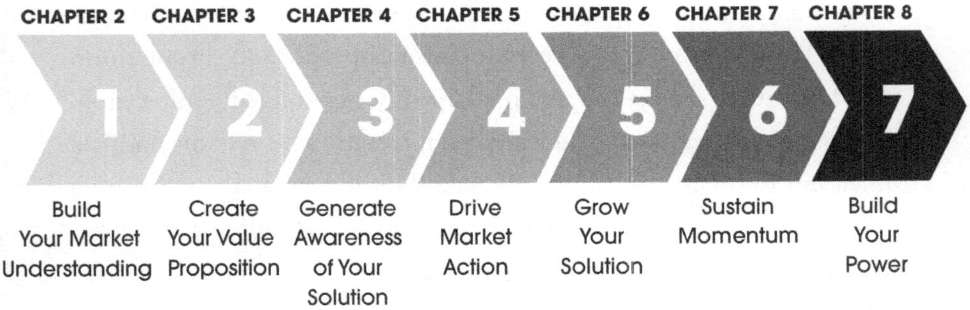

Along the way, we'll dig into the human psyche and learn why it seems like the world is so negative and reactionary. Once you've processed those realizations, you'll learn how to grow your cause from a single person's vision to a fully operating organization capable of being a powerful force in the market.

By the end of this book, you'll be armed with the same growth strategies as the big fish. You'll also have an understanding of how to communicate your message in a way that resonates with your market and can carve chunks off your competition.

It won't be easy, but good things rarely are. So let's roll up our sleeves and get started.

2

Building Market Understanding

DOING YOUR HOMEWORK

You're passionate about change. You light up when you start talking about the future and what could be accomplished if we just generated some collective action. Your enthusiasm and vision are contagious, and everyone you talk to sees the same issue you do, agrees with you on the solution, and wants to help. Sure, there might be rare individuals who don't understand, but these are rational people who will be swayed by the compelling evidence you present of a long-term greater good. No one ever disagrees with you about your solution, or your data, or the fact that a problem even exists.

I'd love for this scenario to be true, but reality tends to differ from this vision. If you find yourself thinking you're going to bring change to a market and all your dominos will fall into place, you don't yet understand the market you're about to enter.

Remember: markets resist change. To give your solution a shot at survival, you will need to identify and understand the market levers you can pull to effect your change. That process is what we call **market research.**

Performed well, market research creates the road map for a successful solution before you commit time and resources so that you have the best likelihood of success. What you're trying to do during this preliminary stage is:

- Determine your idea's viability
- Understand who would choose your solution, and why
- Identify potential competition
- Clarify where your audience can go for information on your cause

This chapter will guide you through the market research process.

CAN YOU SKIP THE RESEARCH?

One of my growth clients has a goal of launching a new product every year or two. Over the years, we've built up a rich library of customer survey feedback on product improvements, service adjacencies of interest, customer challenges, and more. Every year, I lead a survey and focus group to uncover and vet ideas for the next potential product launch, and the process hums along to deliver a result that has helped the company see 40 percent growth rates in the past few years.

It runs smoothly, except for once a few years ago, when executive leadership handed down a directive along the lines of, "We should add this potential offering to the survey."

I've delivered and debated enough research presentations to know that what the leadership team was doing was putting its thumb on the scale to launch an idea that had somehow become a no-brainer to them, without any external vetting whatsoever.

> You may have heard the term "smartest person in the room syndrome" used to describe the kind of bias that occurs when a senior figure voices an idea and everyone else slaps their forehead and says, "Of course!" The idea I was given to vet was going to become the next product launch regardless of the research outcomes (which were not positive).
>
> The product folded in less than a year, because the client skipped (or ignored, really) the research in favor of their own enthusiasm for the internally backed solution.
>
> This is the risk you run when you leave market research behind.

TOOLS OF THE TRADE

Market research covers a few areas:

- **Quantitative research:** Objective data that has been collected at scale, usually through some form of survey tool. Quantitative research helps you answer questions like "do enough people want what I'm trying to offer?" or "what percentage of this group would choose my solution?"
- **Qualitative research:** Subjective opinions collected via individual or group conversations. Qualitative research is ideal when you want to get human reactions to different sets of possibilities, or get more in-depth responses to potential solutions.
- **Secondary research:** Information gathered from secondary sources such as government databases, trade groups, etc. Secondary research helps you understand the work that's already been done in your space, as well as current thinking regarding your solution.

- **Competitive research:** Anything you can find on your competitors through reviews, websites, or even mystery shopping. Competitive research helps you understand what needs are already met and where gaps might exist.

You'll ideally have the time and resources to perform all of the above when building your solution, but that's not always possible. Let the scale and impact of what you're about to do guide your process. Are you about to ask for millions in investment? You'll want your market research to be as thorough as possible. Are you simply looking for a straw poll about whether your idea is worth pursuing? A small qualitative research project might be all you need. And today's AI tools can certainly help at the outset.

CHOOSING YOUR INITIAL PARTICIPANTS

Before you start your research, you'll want to identify whose feedback you want and how you'll reach them. Start by building a rough sketch of your ideal customer, then figure out where you can find them in bulk. In most cases, the people you want to talk to have already assembled in some aggregate that you can access. The following groups are all excellent places to start:

- **Competitor customers:** Anyone who is already using or paying for a similar service will provide an excellent perspective for you.
- **Adjacent organizations:** Trade groups, industry associations, citizens' organizations, volunteer groups, and other aggregations of individuals in and around your cause are an excellent point of access.
- **Local business resources:** Chambers of commerce, incubators, entrepreneurship groups, investors, and other gatherings of business thinkers can provide you with guidance on your business plan, model, and other structural needs.

- **Government:** Politicians, industry regulators, inspectors, and others are a must if you are seeking to operate in a regulated sector or enact political change. Many government programs also support small businesses through grants, challenges, and set-aside contracts.
- **Other interest groups:** You can find local or online interest groups dedicated to almost anything under the sun, from frisbee golf to jurisprudence.

To give your research invitations the best chance of success, I recommend building a relationship with these groups and being open about what you're trying to accomplish. You'll often find that individuals and organizations are happy to offer their expertise to those looking to learn, and it never hurts to sweeten the pot with incentives for respondents.

If you're trying to reach individuals directly, a number of list creation and acquisition tools exist, as well as tools like LinkedIn and SurveyMonkey.

ASSESSING MARKET VIABILITY

As you begin your research, you're going to have a glimmer of a solution and an idea of who might want it, but you still need to vet that hypothesis with as open of a mind as you can. So rather than asking direct questions along the lines of "would you buy my solution?" you'll want to ask open-ended questions that let the market tell you if an idea is viable. That way, you can avoid creating a self-fulfilling prophecy.

The questions below can help.

- What is your biggest challenge [in X space]?
- How are you currently solving that challenge?
- What factors drove that decision?
- Does your current solution fully meet your needs? Why or why not?

- What solution do you wish existed?
- If [your solution] was available, what would you want it to look like?
- Who else could you see needing [your solution]?

When assessing viability, you want to look for the factors your solution will need to succeed. Can you find enough people with a significant unmet need that your solution will help? Or are the people you're talking to generally satisfied and don't see a need to go in another direction? Is the issue causing that need solvable, or would it require boiling an ocean?

One of the best indicators that you have a viable solution is the existence of competition. While competition may feel threatening on the surface, it actually means enough people feel a challenge exists to support a current player in the market. And since none of us are ever perfect, the existence of a competitor almost always means an opportunity to compete.

LEARNING ABOUT YOUR AUDIENCE

While you're assessing market viability, you also want to build your understanding of the people you're talking to. Is your initial hypothesis of who's most likely to take up your cause correct, or do you need to change your thinking based on what you're hearing? You can answer that question by gathering information in four key areas:

1. Demographics
2. Psychographics
3. Pain points
4. Information sources

Demographics

Demographics tell you who your audience is. You compile a demographic profile via objective data, such as age, income, location, web browsing habits, and more. This is the kind of data that tells you what your potential audience can afford, how much they spend on certain categories, how far they're likely to travel to shop, etc. For example, if you're bringing a new recycled cup into the market, which businesses might be most interested in purchasing it? Where are they located, and what are their revenues?

You can usually compile broad demographic information from a combination of census data, along with any number of research studies on media and spending habits by demographic. A good research company can certainly do a custom survey to gather this data for you, and it's quite easy to ask demographic questions in a survey.

Psychographics

Psychographics tell you how your audience thinks. Is your target audience status-driven or more practical? Are they patient or impulsive? Are they more motivated by national or local events? Psychographics are the kinds of things you tease out in open-ended survey questions, focus groups, and interviews by asking why someone made the purchase they did. Answers to that question can give you broad direction toward solving the market challenge you believe exists.

Which brings us to pain.

Pain Points

Like any good doctor, you're probing for pain. Is your potential audience sufficiently affected by an issue to want change? Is their pain acute enough that they are desperately looking for an immediate solution, or is it a minor annoyance they may never get around to acting on?

While every respondent will describe some unique flavor of pain, their issues will generally coalesce around five factors:

1. **Convenience:** Something takes too much time, is too far away, or requires too much effort.
2. **Cost:** Something is too expensive, in time or money. Alternately, something is too cheap to be considered valuable.
3. **Quality:** Current market solutions cannot be relied on, for any number of reasons.
4. **Performance:** Existing solutions do not do the job well, or do not provide what your respondent wants.
5. **Attractiveness:** Current solutions are not perceived as desirable, for any number of reasons (poor perception, negative press, perceived popularity issues, etc.).

These factors will become the core of your solution, which we'll cover more in the next chapter.

Information Sources

As you build your audience understanding, you can significantly help your future communications and media mix planning efforts by asking your audience where they go for information and how they discover new solutions.

These days, the information space is changing incredibly rapidly due to the introduction of AI search. At the time of this writing, Google still leads with approximately 85.5 billion worldwide visits per month, but its search market share has fallen to its lowest level in years at under 91% as AI competitors eat into its traffic.[1] So if your search and generative engine optimization and search engine marketing games aren't up to par, you're already behind.

After Google, however, the information landscape becomes much more fragmented. Think millions of social media channels, forums, streamers, chat apps, review sites, associations, publications, and so on. Any one of these channels could be where your customers find credible, trustworthy information. You just need to ask them, and then be ready to push your message through those channels in the future.

Helpful questions include:

- What news sources do you regularly read or watch?
- Where do you get information about [your challenge]?
- What information do you find most trustworthy (e.g., word-of-mouth, written)?
- Are there any experts or influencers you follow in the field?

COMPETITOR RESEARCH

You also want to discover who else might be targeting your potential audience. Doing so gives you a head start on your positioning by showing you what types of solutions and value propositions have already proven effective in recruiting people to your cause.

Questions to ask include:

- What is the best solution to [your issue] that you've found?
- What are you currently doing to solve [your issue]?
- Why did you choose that service?
- What other offerings did you consider?
- What solutions do your peers use?

In addition to your primary research, you'll also want to do a deep secondary search of your own. The more thorough you are, the better sense you'll gain of what solutions already exist in the market and what unmet needs you might be able to fill based on your subjects' opinions about those solutions.

It can be helpful to organize your competitor research findings into how you believe the competitor approaches their **marketing mix,** otherwise known as the **"Four Ps:"**

1. **Product:** What the competitor offers as its solution
2. **Price:** How much the solution costs (in time or money)
3. **Promotion:** How the competitor talks about its solution, and where it places marketing and advertising investments
4. **Placement (or Distribution):** Where the customer can access the solution

When you're analyzing competitors according to the Four Ps, you're looking for gaps between what your audience research is telling you about their need and the current offerings available to solve that need. Are your focus groups complaining of quality issues or high prices with a competitor? Is a competing solution hard to find or implement? Those are opportunities your solution can exploit.

Product reviews from dissatisfied customers can be an excellent source for identifying these market gaps, while mystery shopping is another good tactic for gaining firsthand experience.

PUTTING IT ALL TOGETHER

Your research process should deliver several outputs:

- A defined **target audience** for your solution
- A rough concept for **a minimally viable product**
- An overview of **existing market solutions** (competitors)
- Initial ideas for your **sales and marketing approach**
- Guidelines for a potential **value proposition**

Let's review each of these outputs.

Target Audience

You began your research process with a rough hypothesis of who might be interested in your solution. After finishing your research, you should have clearly defined demographics and psychographics for the ideal individuals who will join your cause or choose your solution. This is your **target audience** (or audiences).

Organizations will often write an overview of their target audience's characteristics: who they're trying to attract (age, income, geography, etc.), their pain points (which become an elevator pitch), the solutions they need, and why they choose those solutions. This draft can become what's known as a **customer persona,** which serves as a template for some of the brand and customer journey decisions we'll talk about in Chapters 6 and 7.

One last note—it's not necessarily a bad thing to target multiple audiences, but you'll need to consider your available resources. One way to help would be to group your audience into the following categories.

- **Total addressable market (TAM):** Every potential customer if you were to achieve 100 percent market share (which, of course, is practically impossible).
- **Serviceable addressable market (SAM):** The percentage of TAM you can realistically serve with your current or planned offerings, operational structure, and resources. Think of this tranche as your reality check. While it may be theoretically possible to reach the entire United States, you might only have enough marketing budget or volunteer outreach to focus on a few states.
- **Serviceable obtainable market (SOM):** The percentage of SAM you can reach within a specific time frame. This segment is used for business goal planning. If you only have the budget to fund a launch campaign for six months, what would your realistic return look like in that time period?

Let's take a look at a real-world target audience example showing the transition from hypothesis to customer persona based on market research.

Who Buys SUVs?

When you think of an SUV, you likely think of snaking up a winding canyon with a kayak strapped to the roof and mountain bikes lashed to the back. Maybe you envision tearing down a dirt road in four-wheel drive because you need to get somewhere out in the country where the roads end. There are innumerable ads with these kinds of messages, most often with a rugged outdoorsman (emphasis on man) at the wheel.

This idea of the SUV target audience likely goes back to the immediate aftermath of World War II, when companies like Jeep and Land Rover repurposed their existing wartime production models—including the Willys Civilian Jeep, which eventually became the Jeep Wrangler, and the Land Rover Series I—for civilians. Both were heavy duty utility vehicles designed for off-roading and saw strong popularity among returning servicemen. The platforms diversified and softened over the years, but the initial image of a strong farmhand bashing through the fields remained.

If you were introducing a new SUV platform these days, you might be tempted to target the same audience. But your hypothesis wouldn't bear out. Your research would reveal that SUVs account for nearly 50 percent of the U.S. car market, and that 63 percent of SUV buyers live in the city or suburbs. Most importantly, you'd find that women buy 62 percent of all new cars on the road, including 52 percent of all new SUVs.[2, 3, 4]

Now, this might surprise you a bit, and it likely surprised the automakers, too, when they first realized this trend. But if you look carefully at the marketing images, you'll notice the majority actually feature women. The question is why?

You, being a good market researcher, would ask exactly that question during your investigations. And you'd discover that women value safety and utility more than men when shopping for a car.[5]

When compiling your target audience, this is the kind of insight you're looking for. You're not trying to get just anyone interested in your solution, you're trying to identify who is most likely to feel the pain points most acutely and be actively looking for your solution.

For the SUV audience, the need you're actually fulfilling is safety and utility, not off-roading capability.

Minimum Viable Product

Also known as MVP, the "minimum viable product" is a product development concept that originated in the software industry. You can define an MVP as the offering that will generate revenue (or traction toward your cause) with as little effort or investment as possible.

What the MVP gives you is the shortest path to an actual real-world test of your offering. All the market research in the world is never as good as actual behavioral data from your market, especially when it comes to pricing an offering and seeing if your audience will spend money at that price. But it can be hard to decide exactly where you'll draw the line of what you want to provide with your existing resources.

In your research process, the questions you ask about current solutions and the reasons your audience chose those solutions will inform the features or services that need to be included in your MVP. When you're trying to change the world, it can be tempting for you to try to include solutions for every possible challenge you identify. To prioritize, ask ranking-style questions that let your audience tell you what features and solutions are most important for them.

Remember, you're looking to identify the minimum requirements at this point. If your research produces three to five features that you must deliver, everything else becomes secondary when you build your solution.

Initial Sales and Marketing Ideas

Your research participants' insights about how they discover existing solutions in the market represent your first step toward sketching out a sales and marketing strategy. Even if you're working for a cause-driven nonprofit, you'll still have sales (direct in-person contact) and marketing (indirect mass communications) activities to try and motivate your audience. So you'll want your research to give you a preliminary understanding of how to reach the target audience in your market.

Think about ordering your findings in this manner:

- Will mass communications be enough to spur audience behavior, or will individual conversations be required?
- Where does your audience go for information?
- What would it cost for you to have a strong presence in those informational channels?
- What other organizations currently target this audience? Would you partner with them, or are they competitors?

At this stage, you're not trying to build a refined media mix, you're simply giving yourself a starting point for the awareness actions we'll discuss in Chapter 4.

Existing Market Solutions, a.k.a. Competitors

The more competitor information you can include in your research output, the better. We already discussed the critical competitive areas to include, but you may also want to include what's known as a SWOT analysis in your competitive overview:

- **Strengths:** Internal competitive advantages that you possess (or could create) to better position yourself against your competition, such as a more efficient solution to observed market pain.

- **Weaknesses:** Internal challenges you will need to either improve or mitigate in order to compete, such as inexperienced staff or low awareness of your solution.
- **Opportunities:** External factors that could help you succeed, such as a large group of dissatisfied competitor customers or poor overall quality perceptions.
- **Threats:** External factors that introduce risk, such as a dominant competitor who has shown litigious behavior, or an uncertain economic climate.

Guidelines for a Potential Value Proposition

Out of everything discussed in this chapter, your **value proposition** is the most critical component of your market research output. It's so critical, in fact, that we're going to spend the entire next chapter on it.

FINAL THOUGHTS: MARKET RESEARCH WON'T THINK FOR YOU

There's one last point I want to make about market research: it's a decision tool, but it's not a decision. You'll still need to choose how to move forward with your solution based on the evidence it generates. And while research can give you red flags and stop signs based on data such as a lack of market interest, low target audience figures, or high satisfaction with existing solutions, you most likely won't come away from your market research exercise with complete certainty about how to proceed.

Trying to create something new always carries risk. The best thing you can do is identify what an acceptable risk is for you in light of the evidence you have, and move forward.

It's not unusual for decision-makers to demur based on lack of data or clarity after a market research exercise. If you have business-critical questions that must be answered before proceeding, by all means, continue your research. But be aware of "**analysis paralysis,**" which happens when you are overwhelmed by data and yet still feel like you need more information in order to make a decision.

One question I'm often asked is, "How much research should we conduct?" I tell clients, you want to keep your research going until you have data on all your critical deciding factors and start hearing the same answers to those questions. If you do a thorough survey of 1,000 people, those results should give you a high enough statistical significance that adding another 1,000 people likely wouldn't give you much additional value. If you're doing focus groups and start to hear the same answers after your third or fourth group, and your participants are representative of all potential audiences, you've likely plumbed all the knowledge you can.

Case Study: The Curious Case of Nike Considered

Consider the case of Nike Considered. The sustainability-focused Consider line from the world's largest shoe manufacturer caused quite a stir when it launched in 2008, with celebrity endorsements (Steve Nash and Michael Jordan!), press coverage in Outside magazine, and millions of dollars spent to develop sustainable manufacturing processes and tools.[6]

The shoes were crafted from waste materials sourced near Nike's factories to reduce fossil fuels used in shipping, and assembled with a process that eliminated toxic solvents. They were exactly the innovative, sustainable product that consumers claim to want. And then, they disappeared.

Nike gave no reason for pulling the shoes from its lineup, but reading between the lines of post-mortem case studies, it's clear that the shoes just didn't sell.[7] This is an important point for anyone marketing sustainable brands: the largest shoe company in the world, equipped with the very best distribution and marketing support on the planet, put forth an incredible effort to build a truly sustainable product. And it failed.

The question is why?

I wasn't in the room with Nike, so I can't speak directly to specifics, but this case study has all the hallmarks of a product that launched without adequate market research. For decades, Nike has presented its brand as synonymous with elite athletics. In fact, "Just do it" is the exact opposite of "I'm going to make an ethical choice about the products I consume." Because of these factors, it's almost a guarantee that no one in Nike's target audience puts sustainability high on their list of purchase drivers.

From the outside, it sure looks like the folks at Nike were hell-bent on trying to do a good thing for the planet and put their finger on the research scale, just like my client did. Rather than letting their market research guide them, they tried to ram through an idea, and that idea failed.

It's a terrible shame, because the Considered line could have been revolutionary. But it's also the consequence of a lack of market research and a reminder that even the best intentions—and solutions—need to follow the process outlined in this book.

3

Communicating Value

WHY SHOULD I BUY FROM YOU?

If you're reading this book, you've likely spent years working in your industry, researching your cause, talking to people affected by the challenges you see, brainstorming solutions, and lobbying for change. To you, the issue you're trying to solve and the actions needed to do so have become no-brainers.

Now you just need to convince everyone else.

The most important factor to understand when trying to recruit individuals to a good cause is that you must clearly show your audience how supporting your cause will provide them with value. How does your solution solve the pain you've identified better than any other option?

Your answer to that question is your **value proposition**. And a carefully crafted value proposition will go a long way toward helping your cause achieve ultimate success.

What happens if you get it wrong? Let's look at a famous example in the transportation space.

Off a Cliff: How Segway's Poor Value Proposition Doomed the Brand

As internet adoption was taking off in the early 2000s, another revolutionary technology promised to "disrupt" physical transportation:

the Segway. A two-wheeled, self-balancing scooter with a battery large enough to last all day, the Segway was introduced on *Good Morning America* as the future of urban transportation in 2001. Steve Jobs called it "as big a deal as the personal computer," and it could be had for the low price of $5,000 (about $9,200 in 2026 dollars).

The questions immediately poured in: How exactly did it replace a bike or scooter? Could you ride it on the sidewalk? How long did the battery last? Did you need a helmet? And, the most important one of all, who on earth would pay thousands of dollars for something that let them move slightly faster than walking?

The answer was . . . no one. Segway expected to sell 50,000 units in its first year. After two years, it had sold only 3,000.

The reason for this flop was that Segway had no real idea of its target audience, and even less of a sense of its value proposition. The entire company was built to expand the market for inventor Dean Kamen's self-stabilizing gyroscopes, but the self-balancing of the device didn't really solve a need for people who could already balance themselves just fine on a bike or their own two feet. Moreover, the amount of engineering put into safety and redundance features drove the device's price point so high that it was well out of range for most novelty purchasers.

The Segway wasn't really more convenient. It didn't help anyone perform any better, and if you've ever watched a *Paul Blart* movie you know damn well that it wasn't attractive. So what, exactly, was its value proposition?

Today, you'll see e-scooters and e-bikes zipping around most major cities at a fraction of the cost of a Segway, while Segway's personal transporters are off the market entirely and the company is trying to compete with those same scooters and bikes. And, on a tragic note, a Segway malfunction took the life of the company's second owner after Kamen sold it.[1, 2, 3, 4]

This chapter will teach you how to avoid Segway's fate. We're going to start by understanding the importance of unhappiness, then detail the five components of a value proposition that were introduced in Chapter 2 and show how you can incorporate them into your cause from an operational perspective. We'll conclude by looking at a company that's had much better success than Segway in sticking to its value proposition: Patagonia.

FIRST, GET GRUMPY

Remember our Prius example, where we found out that Toyota's intended audience wasn't inclined to spend money on a new car? Another data point the manufacturer uncovered was that the reason why its initial target consumer wouldn't buy the Prius was because they saw the purchase as wasteful. These environmentally conscious individuals were quite happy driving whatever vehicle they owned for as long as they could. To them, large purchases of metal and plastic that ran on fossil fuels were not ones they chose to make often (or at all).

In other words, these individuals were perfectly happy with their current transportation solutions. That was a problem for Toyota, and a version of this issue can threaten your solution's adoption as well. To paraphrase a century or so of socioeconomic thought: truly happy people are bad for business, because they lack material wants.

Your goal, then, is to make as many people as unhappy with the status quo as possible so that they will seek your solution. The cycle looks something like this:

1. Identify (or create) a problem your audience faces (we did this in Chapter 2).
2. Build a solution to that problem (which we'll do in this chapter).
3. Make your audience painfully aware of their problem (Chapter 4).
4. Convince your audience that their pain is so acute that they must act to solve it (Chapter 5).

This might feel a bit cynical for someone trying to do good. But as we learned, people are selfish decision-makers, and most of us will only act when our problem reaches a certain level of intensity. If you believe that the challenge you're looking to solve has passed the point of polite conversation, it's time to grit your teeth and make people unhappy about it.

Look no further than recycling's perennial failure for an example where market pain has not reached enough of a crescendo to compel action.

Recycling

Several studies have identified the reasons people don't recycle:

- Accessibility/convenience
- Time
- Forgetfulness
- Cost
- Lack of knowledge
- Lack of trust[5, 6]

These barriers might seem relatively minor against the backdrop of a collapsing ecosystem. But what's happening under the surface is that would-be recyclers are making a value decision about whether their time and effort is worth the perceived reward of recycling.

Think back to our human motivational theories. How many individual consumers receive any reward for recycling at all? At the time of this writing, just under 22 percent of U.S. states offer rebates for recycling containers, with the highest being Maine at $0.15 per wine bottle.

Are you going to go out of your way for $0.15?

At the same time, what consequence do you face if you don't recycle? No one fines you for not properly sorting your trash, and many municipalities require you to pay extra for the privilege of having a recycling container.

So, when we lament that recycling adoption is slow, what we're really saying is that consumers don't face enough pain to encourage recycling, and they don't receive enough value from doing so.

UNDERSTANDING THE COMPONENTS OF A VALUE PROPOSITION

We touched on the components of a value proposition in Chapter 1. To recap, purchase decisions are inherently selfish—individuals make decisions based on what they expect to receive in return, and want to get the most "value" for the least amount of effort possible (usually measured in time or money).

Of course, different people define value in different ways, so we've got some flexibility in how we present our solutions. With that in mind, you can construct a value proposition out of the categories below:

- **Convenience:** You're saving your audience time or effort and generally making it as easy as possible to solve their problem.
- **Cost:** You're either saving your audience money, or giving them the best value for their dollar.
- **Attractiveness:** You're making your audience more desirable in some way.
- **Quality/Trust:** You're giving your audience strong reliability and dependability.
- **Performance:** You're enabling your audience to achieve something they could not have otherwise done, or helping them meet a certain standard.

Do you know what you don't see here? Words like empathy, altruism, sustainability, or the common good. It bears repeating: as much as they've tried, researchers have not been able to demonstrate that positive social factors can in any way surpass the core five items of a value proposition when it comes to motivating an audience.[7]

If you still want to emphasize the social good of your solution, there's nothing wrong with that. But it's critical that you highlight at least one of the five categories above if you want to avoid Segway's fate. Let's examine each area in detail.

Convenience

How easy is it to join your cause? How much effort will an individual need to make to participate? Will doing so save them any time or effort? Your answers to these questions fall under the concept of convenience.

Convenience defines the level of time and effort someone will need to invest in order to access your solution, and it is frequently the most influential purchase decision factor for a potential customer. The more friction your audience must overcome to reach your solution, the less likely they will be to convert.

Put another way, a convenient offering is the table stakes for your value proposition.

We can frame convenience in several ways, depending on the medium:

- **Online:** How difficult is it for users to register and enter donation information? Completion rates drop with every field you ask.
- **Location:** Are your locations easy to find, or are they an hour away from anything and not found on Google Maps?
- **Speed:** Can you get to your audience more quickly than Amazon, or will you arrive next month?

Your audience will almost always choose the most convenient option unless external pressure from something like regulations or availability tilts the scales. People's desire to receive something as quickly and easily as possible is the reason why Amazon has grown into such a force, and why Google drops the search rankings of web pages that load fractions of a second more slowly.

This makes the convenience aspect of your value proposition incredibly important. Brands in high demand, or those that emphasize luxury, scarcity, or elite quality, can still draw customers. Everyone else needs to be as accessible as possible.

When thinking about how you'll actually deliver your solution, here are a few tips to help you provide a more convenient experience:

- Require as little information from your audience as possible (by, for example, using email appending tools to capture address data).
- Deliver on your promises as quickly as possible by front-loading your rewards.
- Perform as much of the decision work for your audience as possible. Give them straightforward options packages, make pros and cons clear, and provide supporting information.

If we return to our recycling example from earlier, what if our service picked up recycling door to door on a daily basis? Even better, what if we took a page from the milkmen of yesteryears and delivered new product whenever the existing product ran out, while also taking away empty containers to be reused? What if we then cleaned those materials and sold them back to local processors? We'd be solving the issue of recycling compliance at the consumer level, and we'd also be cutting out a laborious and time-consuming aspect that the processors face. This is how you add convenience as a value proposition.

Cost

When an individual thinks of cost, they're considering the question, "How significant is this pain point for me, and how much am I willing to spend to solve it?"

Outside of convenience, cost is the next most influential component of your value proposition because the majority of a market will typically flow to the lowest-cost solution that provides acceptable quality.

However, you have a bit more flexibility in how you position your value proposition around cost.

- **Lowest cost:** Your solution can compete to be the lowest-cost provider, along the lines of Wal-Mart. Remember the recycled cup example at the beginning of this book? That organization clearly felt it wasn't going to spend any more for drinkware. Meaning, the pain it felt at not using recycled cups wasn't even worth a fraction of a penny. If you're operating in a market like this, it's important that you come as close as you can to price parity.
- **Cost savings:** Your solution saves cost in another area. In the example I gave in Chapter 1 regarding the composting client, one of the key issues was that the composting service was initially an additional cost to businesses that were already operating on low margins. As soon as we adjusted our value proposition to show how much we could help those businesses save on waste removal, we were able to turn things around.
- **Quality:** Solutions making claims of higher quality or performance can often carry a cost premium. You'll see an example at the end of this chapter from Patagonia, which is known for its sustainable sourcing, responsible disposal of used clothing, and repair services. What it isn't known for is low prices.
- **Luxury:** At the high end of the pricing spectrum, luxury brands differentiate themselves with high prices that are in themselves a

status symbol. For example, Tesla priced its initial roadsters at an extremely high price point to position the brand as aspirational (and fund further operations).

There are a few other factors about cost to consider. The first is that your audience rarely makes a pure sticker decision. They will weigh the other factors of your value proposition (quality, convenience, etc.) alongside your price to see if they're getting the best value possible. For example, people are generally willing to pay more for convenience, but at a certain price point that desire will fade.

The second factor is that "good" solutions frequently struggle with higher initial price points due to the materials used, more complex manufacturing processes, smaller market, and other factors. Your audience will not have unlimited funds, so it's critical to ensure that your price points can support your value proposition.

The third point is that cost is very frequently viewed as an individual experience, as opposed to a shared experience. If you think about current areas where macroeconomic factors are reflected in high costs, such as climate change, those costs are rarely felt at an individual level. For example, in the county where I'm writing this book, the local government is discussing charging households by weight for their garbage services in order to encourage recycling. All of a sudden, the cost of not recycling appears to be much higher, while recycling could result in cost savings.

Finally, cost doesn't have to be presented as a dollar figure. You can use the concept of losing a deal or a limited-time offer in fear-based messaging, which we'll further detail in Chapter 4. Messages like "What would you lose if something happened?" or "How much longer can you wait?" can be effective with this approach.

Attractiveness

The first quality that comes to mind when you consider attractiveness is likely physical: clear skin, toned bodies, and luxuriant hair, possibly drenched in sun, poolside, with a low-carb beer prominently displayed. And while that's certainly one aspect of attractiveness, your solution can emphasize a number of other factors to appeal to attractiveness.

- **Health:** If you've ever seen a pharmaceutical ad, you've seen a health appeal. We all want to feel as good as we can and live as long as we can, and health appeals that show a carefree individual out for a walk with their spouse can be very attractive to individuals struggling with chronic issues. Other aspects such as water and air quality, the health of the environment around us, and even the mental challenges of living in a blighted area can all be highlighted in a health-focused appeal.
- **Wealth:** Wealth is attractive because it puts an individual in control of their own destiny and potentially allows them to achieve their dreams. Individuals seeking financial freedom and independence will be more likely to gravitate toward messages that emphasize lower costs, putting money back in their pocket, or investing in a solution that generates a return. If you've ever sat through a solar power pitch, the sales rep has likely shown you how much you can save on your electric bill, and how much you can earn by selling renewable energy credits. That's a wealth appeal designed to make the solution more attractive.
- **Public recognition:** Fame carries a certain type of attraction, and the opportunity for public recognition is often a motivator. Think about the volunteer leader who's been recognized for their hard work with an award, or a contest winner, or someone who is honored for their impact on a field of study. These actions help make individuals more attractive in their own small way, even if it's only in the recipients' minds.
- **Power:** Power appeals offer a sense of regaining control over an issue. It's rare that a solution can credibly offer something like political or economic power, but you will often see appeals to

"take the power back" by voting on amendments, or marching in support of a cause.

- **Expertise:** Building expertise can make an individual attractive, because it encourages others to approach them for help and makes them feel wanted. Emphasizing expertise and knowledge is one way to push attractiveness.
- **Aesthetics:** The aesthetics of inanimate objects can be used to highlight attractiveness. Curb appeal, design lines on a car, fabric thread count, and more all emphasize the look and feel of what's being sold, under the assumption that their effects will spread to the owner by extension.

How much weight does your target audience place on any of the criteria above? If they use your solution, how much more attractive will they become?

You have control over these answers, with the potential to leverage everything from peer pressure (think "I Voted" stickers) to improved longevity through better environmental and health care outcomes. The question for you to consider is how much you'll need to emphasize your solution's attractiveness.

Example: Mushroom Leather

A few years ago, I sat in on a presentation from a company that was making vegan leather out of mushrooms. The company was seeking investment to scale up production in order to demonstrate that the cost and longevity of the product was comparable to traditional cow leather. Aside from the novelty of the product, their promotional strategy caught my attention.

They'd landed a contract with designer Stella McCartney, who's famous for her father, her luxury clothes, and her commitment to animal welfare. There's nothing more attractive to some people than a luxury brand, and having mushroom leather clothing showing up in high-end boutiques is a great way to make your solution attractive.

Quality/Trust

We tend to think of quality in relation to the durability of physical goods, like tires for your car. Trust applies more to services, including the garage that installed your tires. In both cases, however, you're striving to emphasize your reliability and dependability. The question a quality- or trust-focused value proposition answers is, "Will I get what I paid for?"

Cost and quality are generally interlinked. If your solution requires a good deal of time or money from an individual, that individual will have certain expectations for how long what you're selling will last, or the quantity that they receive, or how you'll handle any issues that arise. These expectations tend to lower as costs decline, but if you're providing a low-cost solution, improving quality or trust can be the key to outshining your competitors.

As I write this in the post-COVID era, consumers everywhere are decrying a quality decline in everything from food to clothes and furniture, which the media has dubbed "enshittification." These complaints primarily stem from the fact that prices for most goods have risen to levels that previously came with expectations of higher quality.

Trust, on the other hand, is far more complex. The dictionary definition of trust is "firm belief in the reliability, truth, ability, or strength of someone or something." As you can see, trust is far more ephemeral—and far more fragile—than quality.

To earn and keep someone's trust, you must do what you say you are going to do, when you say you're going to do it. In other words, you have to keep your promises. And when you're dealing with challenges at the scale of significant social issues, those promises can be very hard to fully meet (especially if they involve politics).

So, if you are going to make trust part of your value proposition, it's important to stay achievable. "Eliminate cancer by 2030" is a pie-in-the-sky goal, not a promise, but "raise $50,000 for cancer research" is much more achievable.

Incidentally, it's important to align your operations to generate trust. Scandals like those that affected the Wounded Warrior Project or the Susan G. Komen foundation erode trust and damage causes.

Performance

Performance-based value propositions focus on what your solution will help your audience achieve. These claims generally focus on how much better, stronger, faster, longer, etc. your audience will be able to perform (I swear I'm not talking about Viagra, but it's a great example of this kind of value proposition). The point is that you're enabling your audience to achieve something they could not have done otherwise, or meet a certain standard.

If you've ever considered a product that has a "professional" version (iPads, golf gear, software, etc.), these solutions appeal to the performance need of an audience. If you choose the "pro" version, of course you'll be more productive, have a longer drive, etc., than before.

You'll often see performance claims in more specialized product categories, where the product is sold to enthusiasts who are well-educated in market options. These value propositions will often emphasize numeric superiority (zoom ratios, megapixels, etc.) or rank the solution directly against its competitors to show that superiority.

OPERATIONALIZING YOUR VALUE

Your value proposition is much more than marketing copy. It dictates how you'll structure your organization's operations to deliver on your market's needs and differentiate yourself from the competition. Therefore, it's critical to build your MVP and business model around delivering better value than any other market solution in one of the five categories.

(If you're wondering, yes, even nonprofits and causes should adopt this approach, unless you plan to be an unpaid volunteer for the rest of your life).

For example, if your market research identifies attractiveness and convenience as the most important considerations for your audience, you'll need to invest in your logistics and systems to deliver on the market's expectation for convenience while also putting effort into your product or solution design to meet the attractiveness requirement.

One of your initial challenges will be focus. You likely won't have enough resources to meet every audience expectation, so you'll need to choose where to focus the resources you do have to deliver the best possible value. For example, if cost is the most important factor to your audience, you'll need to make a decision on the level of quality and service you'll be able to deliver at a low price point.

Below are two spider charts showing sample value proposition and positioning approaches. The scale is illustrative, but if you imagine 100 representing maximum resources and effort, this visualization can give you a sense of how two different brands approached their solution in different areas.

Example Positioning Charts

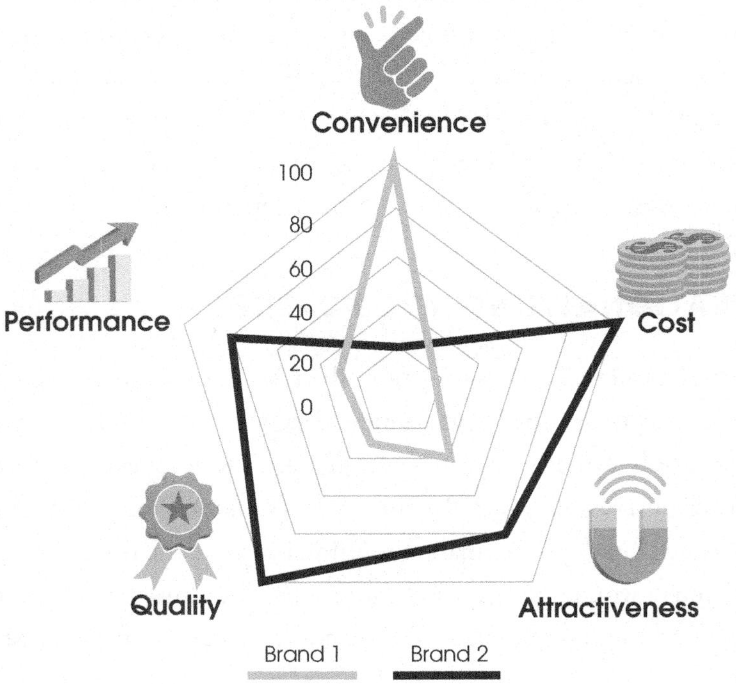

Brand 1 (the gray line) is putting all of its focus on convenience. Maybe this is an impulse purchase, like candy at the checkout counter, and has to be as easy as possible in order to attract business. Brand 2 (the black line), however, could be a custom clothing brand sold at a significant price point. Your audience might need to suffer the inconvenience and cost of going to a store and getting it tailored, but they know they're getting a quality garment that looks good.

Operational focus decisions are challenging, and rarely clear. The process below can help you make your decision.

1. **Model your finances.** Price out everything required to build, market, and deliver your solution. Don't forget to include your own salary and other returns you'll want to see.
2. **Run pricing and funnel scenarios.** Assess where your price will fall in the market compared to your competitors, and then run scenarios based on different adoption and conversion success rates at different price points. The SAM and SOM calculations from your market research will come in handy here: flesh them out with conservative estimates of how many people you can afford to reach with your marketing, what percentage of them will indicate interest, and what percentage of them will convert to revenue. Be conservative, using a 1-3 percent sale conversion rate for your solution, and work backward from that figure to understand how many sales, donations, etc., you'll need, and at what price, to hit your required financials.
3. **Set your price and adjust your value proposition.** The work you did in the previous steps will give you a price range. Now you need to address where that price falls in the market and what your audience's expectation will be at that price. For example, if you find yourself with a higher-cost product, look at how you can support that price with other value proposition components

like money-back guarantees or additional services that would give a better perception of quality. If you're coming out on the lower end, you might have an opportunity to grow even more quickly if you can add focus on convenience.

4. **Plan out your value delivery.** It's now time to put your money and time to work. Collaborate with your team to develop guidelines for how you'll approach and support the areas below:

    - **Product:** What features and benefits must be included in your minimum product? How long will your product be expected to last? If it's a service, are you delivering once or on an ongoing basis? Your decisions here will guide your operational requirements.
    - **Operations:** The production and delivery of your solution is the most critical component to delivering on your value proposition, but you'll have a range of choices here. American-made with fully organic, traceable materials is quite different from something made as cheaply as possible overseas.
    - **Marketing and sales:** How you communicate and deliver value to your audience across your customer touchpoints will be critical to gaining market traction. So critical, in fact, that we've got an entire chapter on it (Chapter 6).
    - **Customer service:** After they've engaged with you, what level of service and support will your audience expect? How much will it cost to deliver that service?

Getting more granular, here are some operational focus suggestions based on the four non-cost value components:

- **Convenience:**
    - Logistics and delivery efficiency
    - Streamlined web interactions

    - Holding more options in stock
    - Easy self-service
- **Attractiveness:**
    - Aspirational marketing messages
    - Use of spokespeople and influencers
    - Product design
    - Customer engagement and retention efforts
- **Quality/Trust:**
    - Third-party quality claims (expert reviews, customer ratings, etc.)
    - Customer touchpoint mystery shopping
    - Customer surveys
    - Human support available on demand
- **Performance:**
    - Independent evaluations and testing
    - Comparative marketing
    - Use of spokespeople and influencers
    - Event and expert sponsorship

Sustainable Performance Value Proposition Example: Patagonia

With revenues approaching $2 billion, Patagonia is one of the largest Benefit corporations (B corps) in the world.[8] B corps devote a portion of their revenues to meeting high standards for social impact, which makes Patagonia a great example of how a company can create a value proposition that allows it to benefit the greater good.

The company began in 1957 when rock climber Yvon Chouinard started making and selling his own climbing equipment, and went through several iterations before opening its first retail store in 1973. Patagonia's mission has long been to build the best product, cause no unnecessary harm, and use business to inspire and implement solutions to the environmental crisis. The company backs up that mission by producing clothing made from recycled sea plastics, auditing its supply chain to eliminate environmental and societally damaging practices, and pushing the boundary of the three R's—reduce, reuse, recycle—even further by taking back its old clothing and offering it for resale as either a discounted piece or a component of a new piece.

These operational choices show a deep commitment to Patagonia's value proposition. But notice what comes first in the company's mission: "Build the best product." Using our value proposition guide above, we could evaluate Patagonia's focus as a mix of quality and performance. The company makes some of the best outdoor gear available, and it stands behind those clothes with a satisfaction guarantee, repair service, and used gear trade-in policy that no other brand can match. This is the definition of a strong value proposition.

Recently, the company changed its mission to "Save our home planet."[9]

This is a lofty goal, and you could argue that a clothing company alone would never be able to reach it. But an organization that focuses first on generating revenue from its audience of outdoor enthusiasts through a strong value proposition is much better positioned to achieve the economic power required to make a difference than other organizations who might go to corporate donors with their hat in their hand.

Case Study: Black Lives Matter

How do you harness a cultural moment and turn it into action?

One of the most interesting social movements of the past few years from a marketing standpoint has been the Black Lives Matter (BLM) movement. The movement originally began as a hashtag in 2013 after the acquittal of George Zimmerman for the shooting death of Trayvon Martin, and exploded in popularity in 2020 after the global protests that followed Derek Chauvin's killing of George Floyd.

The movement generated broad initial popularity, but that popularity quickly ebbed. Two-thirds of Americans claimed support for the cause in 2020, but just three years later, that goodwill had faded, and only half of U.S. citizens approved of the BLM movement by 2023.[10] This decline primarily came from white Americans, fueled in part from opposition groups that used alternate versions of the slogan including "Blue Lives Matter" and "All Lives Matter."

Race is one of the most sensitive topics in the country, and the roots of the BLM movement's grievances run generations deep. For the purposes of this case study, we're going to examine the slogan itself as a means of generating and sustaining movement toward a cause.

Positives

As an awareness tool, the movement generated incredible initial success. The slogan was painted on streets surrounding the White House, and received nonstop media coverage. As a marketing call to action, "Black Lives Matter" creates some very strong positives:

- Clear identification of a target audience
- An emotional plea to an audience that keenly feels a lack of visibility and understanding of their issues
- A sense of potential empowerment

Challenges

Where the BLM call to action struggles is in specificity. To the casual observer who spends a few seconds taking in the message, is it clear what exactly the BLM movement wants to accomplish?

A bit of research will show that the movement is primarily concerned with ending police brutality and societal violence against people of color. Digging a bit deeper brings up a wide variety of other calls to action underneath a very broad umbrella.

The same emotional entreaty that proved so effective in generating awareness proved challenging to distill into a single funnel targeted at driving action.

If we think about BLM as a "product," the movement has done a great job speaking to the pain points its audience feels, but its overall value proposition is vague, due to the significant breadth it is trying to cover. Demanding changes from marijuana legalization to traffic policing to slavery reparations is a very broad platform that makes it hard to understand exactly where attention should be focused and what specific benefits an individual will achieve by joining and supporting the group.

FINAL THOUGHTS: TALKING VALUE

We've spent a lot of time talking about the critical strategic and operational components involved in building your value proposition. In the next chapter, we'll cover ways to talk about your solution so the market will listen. However, please understand that your value proposition is the critical foundation you'll need to ensure the success of your cause.

These details might feel like a heavy slog when you haven't even gone to market with your solution. But I promise that the hard work you do now will make your solution stand out and succeed in the market. All of the flashy marketing in the world can't create a change no one wants. And the last thing you want is to be another Segway.

4

Capturing Attention

WHY SHOULD I PAY ATTENTION?

For every Ice Bucket Challenge that sweeps the world and generates millions of dollars in donations, there are a thousand other pleas that fall on deaf ears. These efforts fail for any number of reasons, including a lack of resources to sustain communications, or reliance on volunteers who aren't able to execute communications strategies. But the most critical factor—and the focus of this chapter—is that their message simply isn't compelling enough to capture attention.

Only a very small percentage of your potential audience will be actively looking for your solution and have the time and receptivity to act the moment they see your message. The vast majority will simply be going about their day without thinking about your cause, and the pain point it solves, at all.

This chapter discusses how to break through a crowded media landscape and audience indifference to capture your market's attention (which we call **awareness**). You know broadly what you want to say to your market. Now it's time to put your message into the most compelling format and use that to increase the number of people whose attention you can capture.

We'll begin with a deep dive into our own minds.

UNFORTUNATELY, WE'RE ALL GOLDFISH

From an evolutionary context, a large part of our species' success has been due to our status as nature's elite information processors.[1] Of all the animals on earth, humans appear to be the most capable of synthesizing sensory inputs into higher-order concepts and acting according to those ideas. In real terms, this means we are quite good at things like planning for the winter, or analyzing and predicting our prey's behavior when we go hunting.

Please give yourself a pat on the back as a member of the human race, because things get a bit dicey from here.

Like any other system, our minds can become overloaded. The more stimuli we receive, the less time we'll have to focus on each individual input. And the less time we have to think about something, the dumber we get.

Imagine walking through the gates of a jam-packed carnival. You'll see hundreds of people, dozens of rides, and lights flashing everywhere. There will be smells of funnel cake and soft pretzels and portable toilets, music from the ice cream truck and the band shell and the barkers, people talking and calling and laughing, and thousands of other inputs. It's impossible to focus on any one of these things for any amount of time, so your eyes will roam the crowds, and your mind will shut down and discard any stimuli that doesn't immediately capture your attention. Some of this is conscious and some of it is subconscious, but it is happening constantly, and it speeds up as you receive more stimuli.

Now, enter the internet.

A small number of very smart people have made the entire carnival of human experience and knowledge available to us with just a few taps. And another small group of people, those intrepid evildoers known as marketers, are spending their entire careers and billions of dollars figuring out how to keep us from ever wanting to leave the warm, glowing confines of the internet.

We are all getting dumber for it.

Global IQ scores have been declining for decades, and the scientists who discovered this trend blame the current information environment.[2] Even worse is the fact that the average human attention span appears to be declining.[3] Which means that, after approximately 5 million years of evolution, many people believe that our species now has the same attention span as a goldfish (although this is likely apocryphal).[4]

For those of us trying to promote a nuanced solution to a complex cause, the situation is even more dire.

When it comes to interruptive media like advertising, you've got anywhere from one to three seconds to capture your audience's attention.[5] If you can do so, your brand or cause will see rewards including increased brand awareness and sales, and a general performance lift.[6]

This is critical, because the typical person sees somewhere between 4,000 and 7,000 marketing messages every day.[7] And we've all learned to tune out much of that circus.

Now, there's some silver lining here. In my opinion, we aren't really getting dumber. Faced with an environment of constant information and stimulus overabundance, I believe we have built a more sophisticated awareness of what constitutes advertising. And that awareness means what we're actually doing is demanding a more immediately relevant message that's deserving of our attention.

Either way, our challenge is to break through to the goldfish.

First, we're going to dig into the current media landscape to understand how the attention economy works today. Then we'll discuss messaging strategies that can reach into the aquarium and stick in the minds of your happy little goldfish.

LET'S NOT GET TOO CYNICAL

The respected Swiss scientist Conrad Gessner cautioned that the modern world's overabundance of data was "confusing and harmful" to the mind. You likely agree with him, and I sure as hell do. There's just one catch: Gessner wrote these words in the 1500s, just after the invention of the printing press, as part of his despair over a project to catalog every book ever written in any language on earth.[8]

Gessner was nothing if not ambitious.

Warnings and concerns about how new technology affects our minds and societies have surfaced like clockwork every time one takes root, and yet we seem to have survived thus far. Writing this book in the dawn of the AI era (entirely with my own ten fingers, I might add), it can be easy to feel caught up in society's impending doom. But in reality, communication tools are created to serve an audience. Social media, AI, and whatever comes next are not an endpoint, but a journey. Our job is to understand the tools that exist and use them to reach our own audience.

In other words, I don't really think things are as dark as a dirty aquarium, and you shouldn't either. We all just need to come up for air every now and then.

UNDERSTANDING THE CURRENT MEDIA LANDSCAPE

The media's business model has always been attention-driven, relying on building a subscriber base through targeted content and then levying a premium to sell advertising to that base. Advertising revenue makes up nearly 70 percent of the typical media company's revenue stream,[9] and in many ways this overreliance on charging based on audience reach has become an albatross around the industry's neck.

Media companies set ad sale prices based on audience size, demographics, and engagement. A publication or website that can demonstrate a larger, more affluent audience that spends more time engaging with its content (think number of pages a user views on a website, as an example) is in a position to command a higher price for its ad inventory.

Of course, ad purchases are also negotiations, and media buyers (the people who make ad spend decisions) also factor in the reach of each media property in their advertising mix. We define **reach** as the total number of unique individuals who see at least one message from a brand.

Reach calculations let advertisers configure spends to ensure that their communications reach as much of their target market as possible over a certain period of time. Reach-based strategies are particularly valuable in commoditized markets, where customer demand is largely static and market share shifts are measured in tenths of a percentage point.

All of this means that, to grow revenue, a media company must grow its audience. This is a steep challenge, because most of us consume media in a hub-and-spoke model where we attach to a few trusted sources and rarely venture outside of those sources.[10] And with only so many people in the world who can devote only so much time to consuming media, media companies find themselves having to capture market share from each other in an astonishingly saturated market. This challenge compounds in the face of falling global population forecasts.

We tend to think of "the media" as a company like *The New York Times* or Fox News. But today's media companies are a combination of content platform, ad network, and service provider, with a dash of production studio supporting individual influencers thrown in. And, as the list below of the five largest media companies in the world shows, they already dominate the mindshare of their audience.[11]

1. **Google (Alphabet Inc.)** is the largest media company in the world, serving 92 percent of all search queries on the web[12] and somewhere between 70 and 90 percent of all digital video views

through YouTube,[13] while also providing the internet's dominant web browser and means of tracking web behavior.

2. **Meta,** the parent company of Facebook and Instagram, sees traffic from approximately 71 percent of internet users every day (3.58 billion people).[14]
3. **NBC Comcast Universal** is the largest US home internet provider and fourth largest broadcaster and cable company in the entire world.[15]
4. **Bytedance/Oracle** is the parent company of TikTok worldwide and in the US.
5. **Disney** owns a number of broadcast, cable, and media properties.

As you can see, these companies already control massive audiences, so the likelihood of significant audience (and thus revenue) growth at this stage of their maturity is quite low.

However, these companies also operate platforms for content creators, who receive a portion of the advertising revenue generated and are incentivized to compete for views to increase that revenue.

What that means is that the media landscape is more competitive than ever before, with more content competing for a smaller pie of users. Consider these statistics:

- Television produces an estimated 88 million hours (about 10,039 years) of programming each year in the US alone, but broadcast TV audiences are declining.[16]
- YouTube is estimated to have more than 100 million channels, and currently delivers 21 percent of all TV streaming content.[17]
- YouTube creators upload 500 hours of video content on the platform every minute, which means 262.8 million hours of programming, or nearly three times as much as broadcast television, every year.
- Podcasters publish somewhere north of 25,000 episodes every day.[18]

This trend has only accelerated with the rise of digital media as the dominant consumption platform.

Remember those thousands of marketing messages people are exposed to every day? They are crammed into every conceivable nook and cranny of the media, to the tune of approximately $500 billion spent by US advertisers in 2022 ($200 billion of which was spent by nonprofits). For reference, the country's largest advertiser, Amazon, spends $21,000 per minute![19, 20]

With digital media accounting for at least 62 percent of all media consumption,[21] the media landscape is dominated by an increasingly fragmented production base that relies more on the messenger as its source of legitimacy.

So, as more content producers fight over a largely static number of viewers, they and their advertisers are pulling out every trick they can think of to gain and keep audience attention. And those tricks are decidedly negative.

YOUR BRAIN DOESN'T WANT YOU TO BE HAPPY

To understand the most compelling media content, we need to accept that our brains don't want us to be happy. Our brains want us to survive.

Psychologists call this phenomenon **negativity bias,** and its core tenet is that humans tend to feel negative emotions like fear and anger much more intensely than positive emotions like calmness and satisfaction. The theory goes that we evolved to fixate on our negative emotions because those emotions helped us survive in our early history.

Consider a group of early humans who constantly worried about finding their next meal. This fretting would drive them to gather and stockpile much more food than another group who chose to spend their summer days resting in the shade. Which group do you think had more food to last them through a harsh winter?

While modern farming and food distribution systems have thankfully helped us leave the concerns of day-to-day survival behind, the way our minds process emotional input has not changed.

Our brains are primed to identify and fixate on the negative, and no one understands this psychological reality better than the good people who own every media property you consume.

In a hypercompetitive online environment that depends on attention to generate advertising revenue, where ownership and shareholders demand ever-increasing returns while every outlet in the world is vying for views, media has become locked into an ever-increasing cycle of negativity because the only way to capture more attention is by amplifying stories of danger and conflict.

In the last 20 years, headlines designed to provoke anger or fear rose by 104 percent and 150 percent, respectively, culminating in 87 percent of US headlines in 2020 being negative. And when we look beyond just news, we find that negative social media posts are much more likely to go viral.[22, 23]

And so, bad news flourishes.

EMOTIONAL CONTAGION AND YOU

At the time of this writing, social media's negative effects are much more widely understood. Many US states and Congress are working on legislation to better regulate the content that appears on these sites, and a number of schools are requiring students to leave their phones outside the classroom.

But we didn't always think this way.

If you've ever heard the term "emotional contagion," you've got Facebook and its devious algorithm testing to thank. One of the first major scandals to hit social media, and what many would consider obvious in retrospect, was that in 2012, Facebook allowed researchers to alter users' content algorithms to show either more or less negative content.

The researchers were testing the concept of "emotional contagion," which refers to our ability to influence each other's moods by expressing our own emotions. The phenomenon had been proven in many studies,[24] but had not been researched in environments that did not involve in-person contact, such as a social media feed.

The results of Facebook's research, predictably, showed that the more positive or negative content a user viewed, the more likely they were to express similar sentiments in their own posts.[25]

However, the results weren't really the issue. The scandal came from Facebook allowing the study to be conducted without telling users that their emotions were being tested. In other words, the largest social media company on the planet was allowing third parties to emotionally manipulate its user base.

While some were shocked at the news of these experiments, others took them as a playbook. Today, we face armies of humans and bots programmed to influence users to express various political and marketing outcomes. This artificially manipulated traffic has reached up to 76 percent of all traffic on X (formerly Twitter),[26] while some broadcast networks controversially required all affiliates and anchors to read from the same centrally generated script to generate the tone of news coverage they wanted to see.[27]

Media companies also present engagement metrics to measure how many people took action on a story (commenting, sharing, etc.). If you've ever wondered if the internet is getting angrier, you're correct, and it's because of engagement.

Content designed to evoke anger and outrage tends to drive more engagement and reactions than any other emotional tone,[28] and comments on most articles tend to skew toward threats and violence due to the anonymity of the platform.[29] Because media metrics (and ad rates) are based on engagement, negative and reactionary content will always be seen as preferable by the owners of those platforms.

This is the modern media landscape you will face as you try to make your voice heard.

IS IT ALL BAD NEWS?

Let's take a deep breath and remember, from Conrad Gessner's example, that society has faced—and solved—its media ills before.

The barely sourced clickbait stories we complain about today aren't new. More than 100 years ago, we called it "yellow journalism," and ever since then, outrage-driven media has been churning along in supermarket checkout aisles and political advertisements. Society has avoided collapse all this time.

It's important to remember that in reality the world is safer than ever before,[30] crime in the US is approaching historic lows,[31] and the US's renewable energy production surpassed coal-based output way back in 2019.[32]

So when it feels like the sky is falling, remember that the media's appetite for sensation means it will overemphasize bad news simply because it is:

a. Something that happened
b. More likely to generate an emotional response

Let's think about car accident coverage. Americans take 1.1 billion motor vehicle trips per day,[33] and if you watched your local news you'd assume we were all crashing into each other with reckless abandon. In reality, only 16,720 vehicle accidents happen in a given day,[34] less than 0.002 percent of all car trips.

But you'll see grisly images of twisted wrecks on a nightly basis, because it's something that happened, and it can generate negative emotion.

Put another way, there can be no "news" if everyone is happy and content. And if there's no news, there's no advertising revenue to be generated.

So let's exhale and understand that what we are shown is designed to elicit a reaction, not reflect objective reality.

YOUR BRAIN DOESN'T WANT YOU TO THINK AT ALL

We've all made gut decisions before. When we do, we're following a vague sense of intuition that we can't quite put into words or explain, so the best we can do is give in to that feeling. That's because your "gut" is shorthand for your emotions, which operate on a level below rational thought and influence our decisions much more deeply than many of us would like to admit.

Researchers believe that up to 95 percent of our decisions are emotionally driven,[35, 36, 37] meaning we are not quite the rational, evidence-based decision-makers we'd like to believe we are. This means media messages and emotional appeals can potentially manipulate the vast majority of our decisions.

Current psychological thinking holds that our emotions evolved as survival tools to help us navigate an uncertain environment where all we had were our wits (and our gut). Emotions likely evolved long before language and rational thought, and because they are survival tools, they will trigger much quicker than the logical portion of our brains. There's no time for talking and thinking when a lion springs out of the savannah.

Yet we make hundreds of decisions every day, and we're not constantly walking around a dangerous jungle in heightened emotional states, fearful of tigers and bears. So how exactly do we make decisions?

Let's reframe our emotions as tendencies toward certain actions, and our emotional state as one of "action readiness."[38]

Over the course of your life, you've educated yourself on certain topics, made choices, experienced the outcome of those choices, and as a result developed a predisposition toward certain decisions. All of that learning has taken a lot of mental processing, and the next time a similar choice comes up it's much easier to respond the same way you have in the past rather than to go back into research and exploration mode.

Put another way, your brain wants to eliminate the processing load that comes with novel stimuli, and it relies on the action readiness created by your emotions to do so. Carrying uncertainty, doubt, or worry is much more mentally and physically demanding than simply reacting and instantly relieving those emotions.

Time is a critical factor here as well. Numerous studies of time-limited decision-making have shown that the less time we have to consider a message or choice, the less time we'll spend actually thinking about it and the more we'll fall back on what we already know,[39] which often time means our gut.

So when we find ourselves bombarded with thousands of messages every day, the majority of which are negative, it puts us in a heightened negative emotional state, making us less likely to think about any single message and more likely to simply react in a familiar way.

This is how generating awareness works:

1. Stories and advertisements are run to generate awareness of an issue or solution.
2. This awareness is designed to create an emotional response in some way (ideally to drive your audience toward one of your value proposition factors).
3. The audience sees enough messaging that they enter a state of action readiness.

WHY FIRST IMPRESSIONS MATTER

If any of this sounds like it describes the current political environment perfectly, you'd be absolutely correct. That's because of the power of **primacy,** or first impressions.

We rarely stop to think too much about the messages we receive, so we rely on trusted sources to prejudge information. The first time we receive information from a trusted source tends to be the most impactful, and cements our viewpoint due to how our minds are wired.

Political advertising, for example, will work to paint an opponent, opposing party, or even a concept with a critical brush for years before an election. That is done intentionally so that the first time you hear about an opponent, it will be negative. That initial impression will then guide you when the time comes for action, and you will vote the way the advertiser wants.

Primacy is so strong that it can cause people to cling to misinformation even more tightly after they receive the truth. A study provided participants with mock news stories, each of which contained misleading claims from politicians and later corrections. Researchers found that people tended to believe the misinformation even more strongly after reading the correction.[40]

This is a real-world example of cognitive dissonance in action, and it shows the importance of first impressions.

4. You put out a call to action, to which your audience responds (ideally without thinking).

The entire goal is to prime your audience with action readiness so they'll pull their decision trigger without thinking. Consumer brands spend billions of dollars to generate awareness around a specific value component so that when you walk into a store without a strong sense of what you want to buy, you'll choose the familiar brand. Their goal is to generate an emotional connection so deep that it becomes part of their audience's identity.[41]

We could sit here and wish the world (and our minds) was different, but in reality the world is the way it is because of our minds. Our job, as agents of change, is to use what we know effectively to make the change we want to see.

HOW TO BREAK THROUGH: TACTICS TO GENERATE AWARENESS

Now that you understand how emotion-driven media operates, and how your audience will respond, it's time to actually put your message out in the market and get attention. To do that, you'll need to build a compelling message that makes as many people aware of the challenge and solution you're promoting as possible, then hammer that message home in a campaign to drive demand for your solution.

Ad researchers have come to a consensus on four commonly accepted messaging tactics to break through the cluttered media landscape:

1. Emotional appeals
2. Scarcity
3. Authority endorsements
4. Humor

Let's explore them in detail.

Emotional Appeals

Remember, you're talking to goldfish. Three seconds isn't very much time to capture someone's attention, but luckily, you've just learned that the less time people have to consider a message, the more they respond based on emotional cues. That's why emotional appeals are one of the most common tools employed to capture an audience's attention.

You've already got a basket of criteria you want to emphasize regarding your value proposition. The key now is to ensure that you communicate those challenges and solutions emotionally. You can do so by using:

- Arousing slogans
- Imagery that focuses on individual expressions (think YouTube thumbnails)
- Emotional music
- Intentional tone (in color palettes, voiceovers, and subject matter)
- Scenes of individuals experiencing your challenge or enjoying your solution

Emotional appeals often focus on imagery over copy, to the point where you may only include a few words. With this approach, you're trying to catch attention, not educate, so your call to action should be designed to bring your audience to a location where they can learn more.

Scarcity

Remember our discussion of fear and greed? A scarcity-based message is designed to make your audience feel like they're going to lose something if they don't act quickly. Your goal is to drive action and reduce consideration time. No doubt you're familiar with some of the most common scarcity-based approaches:

- Deals that will expire soon, such as end-of-month sales
- Limited-time availability, such as fashion styles that are only available for one season
- Small quantities (think sneakers, or collectibles)

These appeals often play on peer pressure, leveraging an individual's fear of missing out to encourage action. When combined with reinforcing content like influencer unboxings, advance reviews, and high-status individuals showing off hard-to-acquire items, scarcity messages work well for cultural or trend-based products as well as price-sensitive items.

Scarcity-based messages may not be effective when introducing your challenge and solution for the first time, but they may be used later, once you've primed your audience for action.

Authority and Endorsements

You're probably familiar with "influencers," be they social media stars, celebrities, athletes, or anyone else trying to peddle something they're paid to promote. Authority-based appeals tap into those trusted spokespeople to deliver a message of endorsement to their audience.

This method of outreach has proliferated on social media due to the nature of individual-driven content, but it seems to be human nature to follow the behaviors of the famous: the first recorded instances of influencers were actually Roman gladiators who endorsed certain olive oils.

Influencer-delivered messages bypass an individual's skepticism and an audience's general tendency to ignore messages from someone they don't know. The hope is that your audience will give your message a few more seconds of consideration and be well-disposed toward your solution because they trust the messenger. Ideally, this approach lets you generate awareness of your message more quickly than in other circumstances.

Endorsement-based approaches do have a downside. Your endorser is a human, prone to changing their mind or misbehaving, and their actions can bring you negative publicity. You're also exposing yourself to accusations of a lack of authenticity, as sophisticated audiences understand that many endorsers do not use the products they tout and often present an artificial lifestyle.

Humor

Humor is another type of emotional appeal, but it stands out because it drives a different audience reaction. Research has shown that humor makes advertisements more engaging and memorable while making the product more likable,[42, 43] which is your goal if you're trying to recruit people to your cause.

However, not all value propositions can support a humorous message, especially when dealing with social issues. Humor is also subjective—what you find funny may fall flat to your audience.

If you plan to try humorous messages, make sure to get outside opinions via focus groups or other means.

NEGATIVE OR POSITIVE?

We spent the first part of this chapter learning about how humans are primed for negative messages. And yet, there's good reason to avoid this approach in your messaging. Let's examine the benefits and drawbacks of adopting a positive or negative tone when generating awareness.

Path 1: Emphasize the Negative

You could take the approach of emphasizing what's wrong to catch your audience's attention. This approach has been used by thousands of cause marketers, including Feed the Children, Greenpeace, St. Jude Children's Hospital, and many more. And studies have shown that it works—individuals concerned about the environment tend to have greater ad recall when exposed to negative messaging.[44]

The challenge with a negative messaging approach is that, even though our brains are highly sensitive to fear and anger, people will eventually withdraw from negative information to protect themselves. In fact, an Oxford-Reuters study found that people around the world are consuming less news than ever thanks to a rising wave of media distrust and concerns about the news cycle's effects on their mental health.[45]

Now, it can be very satisfying to see this data and think that it serves the bottom-feeding doomsayers right to be losing viewers and revenue. But the larger point is that ultimately, negative messaging will burn itself out. It will create withdrawal, pessimism, and apathy over time, and make your audience even harder to reach and motivate.

For those of us who are trying to motivate others to do good over any significant period of time, this means negativity is like a sugar rush. It will give people a temporary jolt, but the crash will follow. Another way of thinking about it is that you might get the first donation, but you won't get the second.

That's why it's best to turn that frown upside down.

Path 2: Go Positive

Over the long term, positivity wins.

A study from *The New York Times* and the Marketing Science Institute found that while social media content that evoked anger or anxiety was more frequently shared, positive content was actually more viral overall,[46] and focusing messaging too much on demotivating emotions can negatively impact response.[47] Additionally, social media scientist Dan Zarrella has shown that positive content is much more effective at getting and growing a follower count, while other research has found that more positive language is more likely to be shared.[48, 49]

So what's our lesson here? If you post positive messages and content about all the good results your cause is generating (as opposed to the challenges it faces), you'll be doing a great job of counteracting the negativity generated in the media, and much more likely to get more people interested in and sharing your content.

You want to tout those wins as often as you can—one study found that a ratio of five positive interactions were required to counteract one negative attitude or behavior.[50] So turn up the volume and let your positive vibes fly!

How to Create Positive Messages

What are some good ways to stay positive? Think fun and personal.

Engaging, humorous, and unexpected content and messages are the best ways to stay positive when you're dealing with real-world challenges. Think of the Ice Bucket Challenge for ALS. While not every effort will go as viral as that one did, engaging with followers and real-world people, celebrating their success, and showing the simple results of collectively doing good will go a long way to making your message stick.

You can also target the four specific emotions research has identified as green purchase drivers:[51]

- **Cherishing:** satisfaction and happiness with our present circumstances
- **Yearning:** an expectation that the future will improve (otherwise known as hope)
- **Pride:** satisfaction with our efforts
- **Admiration:** a positive emotional response to others that drives us to learn more about them and emulate their behavior

These are all emotional appeals as well, but you won't find any negativity in their definitions. These are appeals that focus on improvement, satisfaction, and reward. They reject fear-based approaches in favor of a steadier, warmer tone of improvement.

And while these kinds of messages may not go viral as immediately as negative content, they will provide more success over a longer period of time.

SHOULD YOU TARGET THE HEAD, TOO?

We've spent a lot of time talking about targeting your audience's heart. What about their head? Do intellectual appeals have the same resonance?

While research has consistently shown that emotions drive decision-making,[52] some evidence does exist that appeals based on statistical or rational information do help increase donations.[53]

When we consider how to frame our value propositions, what this research means is that we can use the emotional component of our target audience's pain point to capture attention and follow up with supporting evidence to compel action.

For example, if you were working on an appeal to reduce waste, you could lead with an image of a child wading through a landfill to capture attention and then support that point with notes about how much waste is generated every day, how much your solution reduces that problem, and how much it costs.

Use emotion to capture attention, and rationality to guide your audience once you have their attention.

Case Study: Solar Power

A few years back, my company worked with a solar installation company to help them grow their lead base. Solar power has always been an interesting case study because much of its appeal rests on the intellectual promise of paying a significant amount of money up front to gradually reduce a relatively small monthly bill. At its heart, the appeal of solar is economic, which is difficult to turn into an emotional appeal, especially when the questionable aesthetics of the panels (compared to traditional rooflines) come into play.

You could argue that this purely rational appeal is one of the main reasons solar power has a difficult time gaining traction. It is primarily an investment, which most people take time to consider, and comes at a higher cost.

So, if you were selling solar power, you may want to focus on the emotional aspect to get attention: "Never pay an electric bill again!" "Cut loose from your gas company!" "Achieve energy independence!" These kinds of slogans can drive a response, which will then open up your audience to be more receptive to the details.

For this client, an interesting fact we discovered was that the most significant factor in an individual's solar power purchase decision was whether a friend or neighbor had it installed. With this data, the value proposition component we wanted to emphasize was actually attractiveness: look at what your friends and neighbors are doing, don't you want to be a part of the movement?

APPLY DIRECTLY TO THE FOREHEAD: THE BENEFITS OF REPETITION

When it comes to awareness, one impression is never enough. No matter how good your messaging will be, there's still no guarantee anyone will remember it even if you're lucky enough to get it in front of someone. That's where repetition comes in.

"Ad recall" is the term marketers use for whether a person remembers a message or not. Once someone recalls your message, if they can remember what company it was for, you've now established **brand awareness**. Massive global brands like McDonald's and Coca-Cola have ridiculously high brand awareness ratings. The rest of us have to work hard to build that equity in our audience's mind.

And that equity has value. Remember, our brains don't want us to think at all. They are always looking for shortcuts to reduce processing power, and the biggest shortcut of all is trust. The typical individual in your target audience is trying to make decisions quickly and move on with their lives. Maybe you want a different type of cereal when you go to the supermarket, but do you really want to spend an extra five minutes in the aisle, reading the labels and checking prices? This is the value of brand awareness.

That awareness becomes even more valuable when we consider the thousands of marketing impressions an average person sees each day. How many of those advertisements do you think actually register?

On the high end, your target audience might recall one-third of the ad messages they see.[54] On the low end, that number ranges between one and zero.[55]

What does this mean for your communications strategy? How do you build brand awareness? It's simple: You repeat yourself, over and over. You repeat yourself until you mumble your slogans in your sleep. You repeat yourself until you, your team, your vendors, and your customers are sick of it. And then you keep repeating yourself, because there are still people out there who haven't heard your message, and because it works.

The magic number for effective recall of an ad is ten exposures.[56] If you go with the high-end exposure estimate of 10,000 messages a day, and the low-end recall estimate of one per day (to be generous), that means you will need your audience to see your message at least 100,000 times to make a dent.

Again, if you're Coca-Cola, you can pull this off easily. The rest of us will have to focus on where we can afford to build that repetition.

Some of the most affordable channels are:

- Google's display network
- YouTube
- Email
- Meta

The Joys of Meeting Repetition "HeadOn"

If you found yourself staying up late or watching reruns around 2006, you probably saw a commercial that was widely considered one of the worst ever made, for a mysterious product called "HeadOn." The video featured a woman applying what looked like a large tube of lip balm onto her forehead and a voice repeating a two-line instruction over and over: "HeadOn. Apply directly to the forehead."

HeadOn's manufacturer chose this shocking, bold repetition after its focus groups demonstrated effective recall for repetitive advertising. The company was seeking to grow reach in the most affordable way possible, thus its media strategy of buying affordable ad slots with an incredibly repetitive message.

Funnily enough, the strategy worked, generating strong sales and a number of parodies that grew the campaign's earned media value.[57]

FINAL THOUGHTS: WHAT DO YOU WANT ME TO DO?

If you're lucky, you've generated awareness of your solution in some significant portion of your target audience. It's a challenging battle, one that takes time, so the most important thing you can do is consistently execute your communications plan and ensure you're driving as much reach as you can. Look at your data to identify the most engaging executions, and revise your messages as necessary. As long as the numbers are moving in the right direction, you'll start to gain traction.

That traction will need somewhere to go. Remember, you've just whipped your audience into a heightened state of action readiness (known as **demand generation**), and they're waiting for you to tell them what to do.

Now it's time to get them to act.

5

Generating Action

WHAT'S IN IT FOR ME?

Once you've captured people's attention, what happens next? As much as we'd like our audience to immediately join us on our march to change, action isn't instantaneous. Your audience isn't waiting idly for your solution to drop in their lap. They are actively pursuing their own priorities, being bombarded by competing messages, and seeking out other solutions the entire time you're trying to convince them to make the change you're seeking.

After you gain your audience's attention, you still have a lot of work to do in order to push them toward a full commitment. As a result, you'll need to stay in continual conversation with everyone who learns about you in order to compel as much of that audience to act as possible.

We call that process **"nurturing."** Nurturing uses **calls to action** to move your audience through their **decision-making funnel** quickly and efficiently. At a high level, the steps in your audience's decision process look like this:

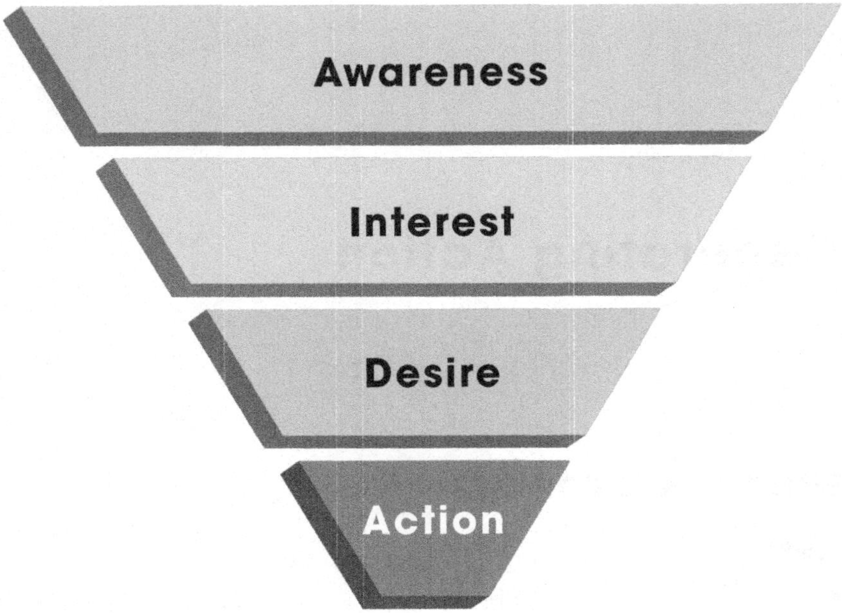

1. **Awareness:** Your audience is made conscious of their problem and your solution.
2. **Interest:** Your audience expresses some desire to learn more about their problem or your solution (submitting a form, contacting your staff, etc.).
3. **Desire:** Your audience evaluates your value proposition against their needs and, hopefully, realizes your solution will best solve their issue.
4. **Action:** Your audience makes a commitment or purchase, or completes some other measure of success for your cause.

You've likely heard of this AIDA model before, or another variation with slightly different steps. While the specifics will vary, and no model exactly matches real-world experience, this framework will help you define the specific actions you're asking your audience to take during their decision journey.

This chapter will show you how to nurture your audience through their funnel by providing communication and education at each stage that moves them to act. So let's put a match to paper and light the world on fire (in a good way, not the global warming way).

UNDERSTANDING THE DECISION-MAKING FUNNEL

Let's start by examining the AIDA model in more detail:

Awareness

Chapter 4 discussed ways of generating awareness, so we'll focus on measurement and action here.

Measuring Awareness

Awareness can be challenging to quantify and track, but it's important to assess whether your efforts thus far are working so you can pivot if necessary. Organizations with the resources to do so will commission recurring research studies to objectively measure how many people can recall their name, with or without context (known as **aided** or **unaided** awareness). If you're operating at smaller scales, you can use proxy metrics like Google search impressions for your solution's name, AI visibility reports, website traffic, social reach, and more.

Action: What Comes Next?

After you've captured your audience's attention, it's critical to know what the next step is in their journey. Ideally, you'll have a low-risk preliminary step that your audience can take in order to identify themselves as potentially interested in your solution. When they do, they've moved to the next stage of their decision funnel.

Interest

Your goal at this stage is to capture some signal that your audience has expressed interest in your solution. Interest can be expressed in many ways: submitting contact information, taking an action on your website, expressing a need to a third party, and more. Regardless of the specific action, you'll want to accomplish two things to move your audience from "aware" to "interested":

- Collect contact information that lets you begin a proactive conversation with that individual
- Build a favorable impression of your organization in your audience's mind (through an easy process, speedy delivery, white glove customer service, etc.)

In an increasingly privacy-focused environment where your audience is growing more reluctant to share contact information, capturing interest has become more challenging. Here are several options you can try:

Third-Party Interest

Both on- and offline, third-party interest generation can be a significant opportunity (that often comes with a cost). Third parties can include existing associations, conferences and events, industry brokers like a real estate website or Angi (formerly Angie's List), or any number of review websites that charge for listings and advertising. They are often your audience's first stop when they begin a research process.

Indeed, Google has stated that in a business-to-business context, the average person conducts 12 searches before navigating to a brand's website.[1] What sites are they pulling up in those searches? Social media sites, review sites, and any number of blogs and influencer pieces (in addition to a flurry of ads).

These third parties build their business model on monopolizing awareness in order to sell leads to the highest bidder. Because of this approach, it is likely worth investing in some of these opportunities (including Google advertising) in order to capture interest volume, especially if you don't have the resources to get to the top of the search rankings on your own.

Be aware, however, that third-party interest is often less "qualified" than people who have sought you out directly.

First-Party Interest

Anyone who contacts you directly expresses first-party interest. You can use a variety of tactics to convince your audience to submit their information to you, including giveaways, educational materials, contests, tools, and other incentives. The best choice to capture interest is often to give something to get something, because it plays on motivational expectations. And the more you offer in the initial value exchange, the better first impression you'll make.

Also, the less information you ask for up front, the higher your lead capture rates will be. Avoid asking for every little detail at the beginning of your interaction, and focus instead on smaller pieces of information (like an email address) that you can use to present further qualifying opportunities to your audience.

Once you receive an individual's information, they've become a **lead**. You can use the number of leads generated to understand how well your awareness efforts perform, and the contact information lets you follow up with them proactively to further nurture them down the funnel and see just how interested they are in your solution.

Desire

Do your leads actually want to join a cause? Do they want to join your cause? We don't know until they provide some indication that they are approaching an action. That indication is what we call the "desire" phase, and could also be thought of as a sales-qualified lead.

Remember that the funnel is not a straight line from awareness to action. Your audience will take a number of actions throughout their journey as they research their options. These actions include:

Intent

Your audience's activities up until now could be considered "shopping around." When you get to the desire stage, it's time to see just how serious they are about solving the problem you've outlined and joining your cause. You do that by evaluating intent, which can be done in a variety of ways:

- **Market research:** When you conduct your market research, ask questions about the time it takes your audience to make a decision, and what criteria they would need. This data gives you the ability to estimate how strong your leads' intent may be.
- **Questionnaires:** You'll get the best data straight from your leads by asking qualifying questions at the point of capture or in follow-up communications:
  - When are they planning on acting?
  - What information do they still need?
  - What barriers exist?
  - What current solutions are they using, and when do those expire?
- **Qualifying actions:** Plan to have multiple calls to action that allow a lead to express their readiness for a next step. Maybe you have a savings calculator they can use, or a tool to apply for financing. Using these features can indicate a greater likelihood to act, and will help gauge intent.

Once a lead provides intent signals, we typically call them a **marketing qualified lead.**

Consideration

A lead who is actively examining potential solutions is going through a sub-phase we call "consideration." Marketers define a lead's potential group of solutions (or products, or competitors) as a "consideration set." The consideration set is a loose grouping that is heavily influenced by the lead's awareness, and will get whittled down in the next sub-phase.

Let's think about a car purchase. If you're in the market for a vehicle, you can probably name a few makes off the top of your head to start with. You haven't fully formed an opinion or researched the options available, but your consideration set will serve as your starting point.

When you perform your market research, questions like "Have you had [problem X] before? What solutions did you consider for it?" or "What solutions would come to mind if you had [problem Y]?" are tools you can use to uncover your audience's most common consideration sets. You can then break down those competitors' marketing strategies to see where and how they are successfully generating awareness.

Remember that your target audience will constantly evaluate their options in the greater marketplace of ideas during their consideration activities. Your audience will also add new solutions to their consideration set as they become aware of them, which underscores the importance of continually running awareness-generating communications and marketing.

Evaluation

As your audience becomes more serious about their choice, they will move into the "evaluation" sub-phase. At this point, they are seeking more information and detail about their initial consideration set in order to identify the best solution for their need. This detail will include first- and third-party information on the specifics of your value proposition and the Four Ps we introduced in Chapter 2. We've covered many of these elements before, but the salient items for your audience may include:

- **Cost:** What is your initial price? Are there ongoing maintenance or other fees?
- **Time commitment:** How much time will an individual need to devote to your cause? Are there levels of commitment?
- **Reward:** What will your audience receive in return for their decision? What promotions exist during their evaluation phase?
- **Features and options:** What are the specifics of how your product functions?
- **Organizational profile:** Are you a new organization? What causes do you support? What position in the market do you occupy?
- **Reviews, certifications, and testimonials:** What do third parties say about your organization and your solution? How do you compare to others offering similar solutions? What sets you apart?

You can help your audience through this stage by presenting the above information in your nurturing communications. Your goal is to support and encourage their decision to choose you by easing any concerns they may have and making the next step as easy as possible.

The reason we spent an entire chapter on developing your value proposition is that it makes your audience's evaluation of your solution so much easier. The more compelling your solution appears against its competitors, the more likely you'll be to break through and drive action.

You'll need to continue your nurturing efforts at all three subphases of the desire stage, but you will rarely have solid information about exactly where an individual stands in their decision journey. For that reason, it's a good idea to provide a number of calls to action before your audience reaches their final decision, in order to capture desire signals that can help you move a lead through the qualification process.

These actions may include:

- Low-commitment volunteer or donation opportunities
- Free educational content (downloads, webinars, etc.)
- Awards and contests
- Informational/Q&A session with an expert
- Surveys
- Deals and discounts

The specific method can vary. Your goal is simply to give your audience enough incentive to show they are still interested or willing to take the final step toward action.

Speaking of which, let's move to the last stage in the funnel.

Action

Your moment has arrived! Your audience member has taken the plunge and become a customer, or a volunteer, or a donor, or any other classification that means they're using your solution. Congratulations, you've converted another evangelist to your cause. Take a minute to celebrate, and then get back to business, because the reality is that the real work has just begun.

Our next step is to retain and grow our relationship with that customer, which we'll further address in Chapter 6.

First, let's look at the specifics of how exactly you can get your lead through the funnel.

WHAT MOVES PEOPLE? CREATING EFFECTIVE CALLS TO ACTION

We started this chapter by describing the journey your audience takes to generate action. Now, it's time to understand how you get them to act. The tool we'll use is your **call to action** (CTA).

After the headline, or email subject, or other attention-getter, your CTA is the most important piece of any message you send. It is how you encourage your audience to make a commitment to your cause based on the promise of a reward. If the rest of your messaging has done its job, your CTA will focus on your promised experience (and value proposition). As such, it is your first step to building trust for your cause—remember the importance of that first impression!

Traditionally, CTAs are quick and punchy: "Donate," "Sign up," "Join us," "Help," etc. They should be the visual focus of your creative assets, and the most prominent copy after your headline. These aren't just suggestions, they're the results of the heavy amount of research marketers have put into driving action.

That research has found that when constructing your CTAs, using some mix of the approaches below (and testing them against each other) will give you the best chance for success:[2, 3, 4]

- **Action orientation:** Beginning your CTAs with an action verb (start, join, etc.) generally drives better engagement than other methods.
- **Specificity:** If you have the space, being specific often generates stronger engagement. Think "Join next month's volunteers" as opposed to "Sign up."
- **Urgency:** Scarcity is an awareness tool, and the same principle applies to CTAs. "Act now" will typically perform better than "Join us."
- **Incentives:** Providing a clear reward in your CTA, such as "Register for your free gift," can help move the needle where "Register" on its own might not.
- **Social proof:** Everyone loves to be on the winning team, so why not show your audience they'll be joining one? Examples would be "March with 10,000 others this July" or "Try what 4,000 other leaders already know."

- **Personalization:** The more personalized your appeal, the more research shows it will drive engagement. Think "We can cut [your address]'s energy bill by $200 a month when you switch."
- **Curiosity:** We all want to learn more about our interests, but "Learn more" is often a weak converter. Try lines like "Find out how," "Learn the secret," and other insider-type appeals in your copy.

Calls to action are not always easy, since you're trying to distill everything you've worked on into a few words. Let's see how other organizations have structured their CTAs to help you build your best motivational message.

Example CTAs

Let's look at several calls to action related to a single topic.

I've chosen climate change as a more challenging example on purpose. Imagine an audience of individuals pulled in dozens of directions, who are mostly well-meaning but not yet feeling the problem climate scientists have been warning of for decades. What can one person realistically do about climate change? What steps can they take that will solve the problem? It's very hard to know, and that lack of clarity just adds to the angst these individuals are feeling (remember how messaging works—we've all been emotionally primed by a generation of media to know that global warming is a significant problem, and it's time to act).

Here are three organizations' campaigns.

Union of Concerned Scientists: "Invest in a Climate Resilient Future"

The Union of Concerned Scientists' call to action asks us to invest, which is slightly passive, but does convey the expectation of a return, albeit over

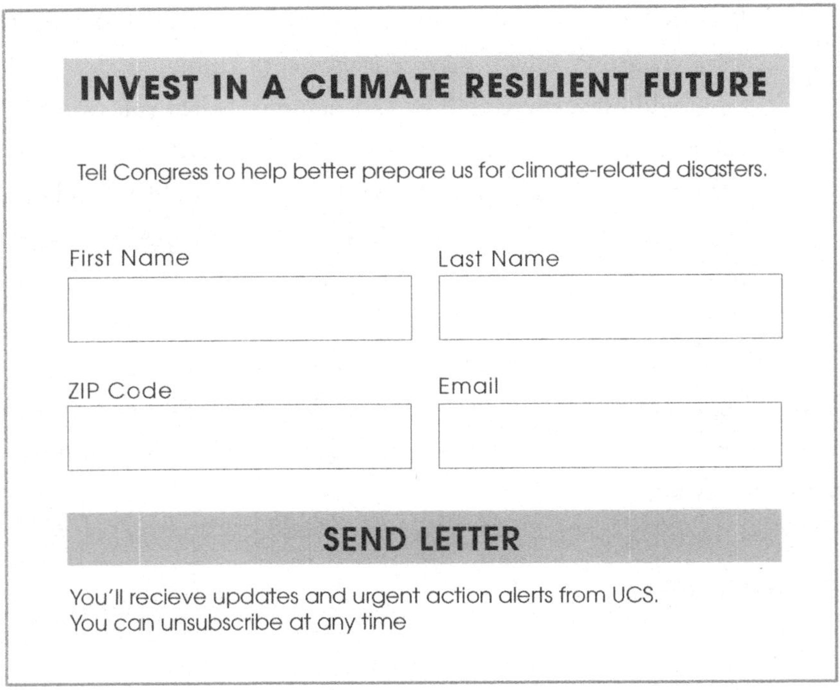

an uncertain time frame. What would that return be? Something called "climate resilience," which has become a more achievable talking point as scientists have seen warning sign after warning sign pass in the rearview mirror.

The "Send Letter" button text is nice and punchy, but to me, this CTA struggles as it doesn't clarify the organization's goal or the return an individual will receive. Sending a message to Congress feels almost futile in this day and age, so I have to believe that an individual's expectation of success here will be quite low.

What could the alternative be?

Perhaps the organization's messaging could involve investing in companies that are delivering climate change solutions, or contributing to the campaigns of politicians aligned against fossil fuels. In both cases, you'd be able to show more demonstrable progress over time and your audience would enjoy a more tangible reward.

Polar Bears International: "Without you, there is no them"

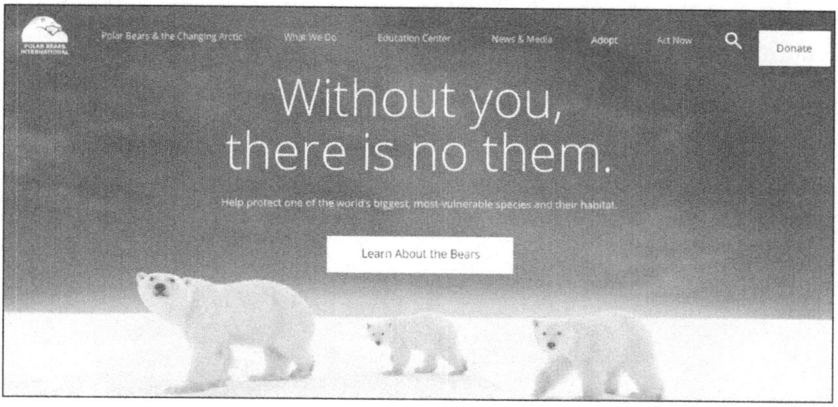

Polar Bears International's mission is to conserve polar bears and the sea ice they depend on, which requires direct action on climate change and global warming. The organization has two main calls to action in the image above: "Donate" and "Learn about the Bears."

While the organization does a good job of publishing impact reports that discuss what they've been able to accomplish each year, there is no stated metric or objective that a volunteer or donor would be able to see themselves attach to and push to completion.

We could improve this campaign by changing the CTA to reflect a goal of purchasing breeding grounds, or helping reduce greenhouse emissions, or other tangible actions that the funds would support.

Note that we've got a "Learn" CTA as the core visual element, which tends to be weaker than action-oriented copy. What if we replaced this copy with "Discover Our Polar Secrets"?

Cash for Clunkers

Our third CTA example became the colloquialism for the U.S. government's 2009 Car Allowance Rebate System.[5] This program had a dual purpose of stimulating the automobile industry during a challenging economic period while also improving motor emissions. It was so successful that the program depleted its funds in two months before being reauthorized by Congress.[6]

What I like about this CTA is that it immediately tells its audience (owners of older cars) what they will receive (cash). That audience doesn't need to know that the program they're using was designed to improve air quality while providing jobs. But they do know exactly what they'll get if they participate. It's about as pure of a match between a value proposition and a CTA as you'll ever find.

GREASING YOUR CAUSE FUNNEL WITH SOCIAL MOTIVATION

Now that we've covered the stages of your audience's decision funnel and spent some time on how to motivate them to act, let's zoom out a bit and see how we can make your efforts as effective as possible. If you've read Chapter 4, you probably won't be surprised to learn that emotion can be the most effective grease to work with. How you choose to deploy that emotion matters.

Remember how major theories of human motivation don't really cover altruism, or environmental concerns, or sustainability, or better governance, or any of the thousands of issues we're struggling with today?

We might have cause for a bit more optimism, thanks to a few intrepid sociologists and psychologists conducting research in an area known as **social motivation**.

Social motivation explores the reasons why individuals choose to actively work toward innovations that benefit the common good, as opposed to more self-centered pursuits that might bring them more individual success (measured in money, fame, etc.).

If you're reading this book, you're likely one of the individuals these scientists study. You could be a government worker, community leader, social entrepreneur, volunteer, or supporter of any cause. And you've likely made some income, lifestyle, or time sacrifices to do so. The question is why you chose the path you did, and how you can convince a broader swath of the population to join you.

Researchers believe that social motivation comes from a blend of three factors:[7]

- **Idealism:** This mindset places values and principles above practical concerns, and weighs an action's impact based on how it might affect others. Idealists are in many ways believers—they have bought in to the possibility of a better system, and instead of being reward-driven, they derive motivation from the satisfaction of their efforts to bring about systemic improvements.
- **Concern:** Does your audience care about your challenge? Are they aware of the problem as you see it, and interested in becoming part of the solution? If so, they have expressed concern. Much of what we've discussed in this book is aimed at improving your target audience's level of concern, and I would argue that concern is the most critical component of a successful funnel campaign. Remember, you are trying to push your audience into a heightened readiness for action, and you do that by elevating their concern.
- **Past experience:** An individual's prior experience with your cause is a large factor in their motivation. If they felt a positive social value and reward from others, that will help maintain momentum for them to lend support at the next opportunity. Think of little cues like the "I voted" stickers you see on election day—it is a simple, inexpensive badge that people wear with pride, and it helps raise awareness and build a sense of community.

When you're communicating with your leads, you want to present information and offers that speak to the motivational components above in order to move them through your funnel.

Case Study: International Bird Rescue and the Marine Mammal Center

When an oil spill affects coastal wildlife habitats, International Bird Rescue (IBR) and the Marine Mammal Center (MMC) fly to the cause. These organizations focus on cleaning and rehabilitating wildlife that would otherwise perish from the effects of losing the ability to fly and find food due to the harmful effects of oil. They are also primarily volunteer-staffed, with resources very driven by the news cycle.

Procter & Gamble's Dawn dish soap touts itself as tough on oil, gentle on skin (and wildlife). As a result, its brand value proposition aligns with the IBR and MMC's mission, and Dawn has been donating its product to its partner organizations for 40 years.

To raise awareness and increase donations, Dawn has partnered with the IBR and MMC for a number of campaigns. These campaigns typically include celebrity representation from individuals like Rob Lowe, Jennifer Hudson, and Kate Mara; a series of educational videos and social content; and actions participants can take to support the IBR and MMC.

For the fortieth anniversary of the wildlife partnership, Dawn funded a media event that included an exhibit in New York's Grand Central Station, a national media day, and a social media engagement push.

While this effort generated strong engagement during its promotion and improved awareness of both nonprofits, IBR and MMC also benefited from a contest where more than 6,500 individuals signed up to win a trip to the organizations' facilities and a chance to go behind the scenes of their rehabilitation operations.[8,9]

While IBR and MMC can't count on having the full weight of Dawn's PR efforts behind them every day, they are able to stay in constant contact with those 6,500 contest entrants, growing their lists and keeping those individuals warm with qualifying actions like small donation requests until the next call for volunteers arrives.

FINAL THOUGHTS: TESTING AND MEASURING

No campaign plan survives contact with the market. When laying out your funnel and messaging, understand that your efforts should best be seen as a hypothesis instead of a final product. The data you capture about response rates, customer segments, and message engagement will dictate your final direction.

It can help to organize your messaging into different buckets. For example, group your emotional content and your rational appeals in different segments to see which performs better. Test these approaches in different media with different audiences to see what you learn.

All of this takes time you might not feel like you have, but it will be worth it in the end.

Because if you can turn your leads into active participants, you now have a supporter for (what we hope is) life.

In the next chapter, we'll dig into that audience life cycle and make sure they do stay with you for as long as possible.

6

Improving Engagement

WHAT (ELSE) IS IN IT FOR ME?

The moment you start to drive action among your audience, it can be tempting to take your foot off the gas pedal and celebrate. But you can't rest on your laurels just yet, because generating initial momentum and keeping your audience engaged with your cause over time are two vastly different things.

Estimates for contact decay, known as **churn,** range from one-quarter to one-third of an organization's contacts in a given year.[1] As the people you worked so hard to capture leave jobs, change email addresses, unsubscribe, move away, and otherwise threaten to slip out of your reach, you'll need to do everything in your power to keep them engaged.

Why? Because it costs anywhere from five to twenty-five times more to acquire a new customer than to retain an existing customer.[2] So if you're not keeping enough of your audience engaged and helping you grow, you're shrinking. And once you start shrinking, it will cost you even more to restart your growth.

It can be tough to keep your audience mobilized and motivated, but it's a critical component to your success. Solving large, complex challenges takes sustained attention, effort, and contributions. The individuals in your audience will face constant demands on their time that could pull them away from your influence at any moment. Health concerns, family issues, more pressing consumption needs, and competitors with much deeper pockets are all vying for your audience's attention, and it's not uncommon for them to win.

This chapter will introduce the latest retention and engagement theories to help you survive and thrive over time in the battleground for attention. They will help you keep your supporters as engaged as possible so you're not trying to constantly plug holes in a leaky retention boat.

First, however, we'll need to spend a little time with the angels.

SPREADING THE GOOD WORD: THE IMPACT OF EVANGELISTS

Have you ever tried a product or service that left you feeling so good you had to tell someone else? If so, you became a marketer's dream: a **brand evangelist.**

Brand evangelists have also been called net promoters, raving fans, enthusiasts, influencers, and any number of other terms that describe someone who spreads positive word of mouth about an organization.

Nearly 80 percent of customers are influenced by positive word of mouth,[3] while more than 90 percent of consumers trust recommendations from friends and family far more than any advertising.[4] McKinsey research shows that positive word of mouth makes someone 50 percent more likely to purchase from that brand,[5] and dozens of other studies show how much evangelists amplify other promotional efforts.

In an environment where peer selling and social media sharing stands a much better chance of generating awareness than advertising, motivated evangelists can drive customer action and engagement like no other channel (and often at a much lower cost). If you ask, they can do the work of finding other supporters for you and give you invaluable feedback when you're looking to refine your value proposition, all because you've given them a fantastic experience.

Brand evangelists represent a unique opportunity for cause marketers, whose entire goal is to create a culture that shares the value they're trying to create. The more people you can convert to your cause, the better your chances of creating a snowball of change that turns into an avalanche.

But creating these cause evangelists is extremely difficult. It's not enough to simply deliver on your promise. You need to wow people and keep them wowed. If you can deliver on the recommendations in this chapter, you'll have the best chance at joining other successful organizations whose customers and participants shout their virtues from the rooftops.

BUILDING YOUR RETENTION STRATEGY

Your communications don't stop once someone converts to your cause. As we learned, audience engagement and retention are just as important as acquisition, and researchers have put some serious science behind them. Parsing through these theories gives us a five-step engagement strategy: Let's address each step.

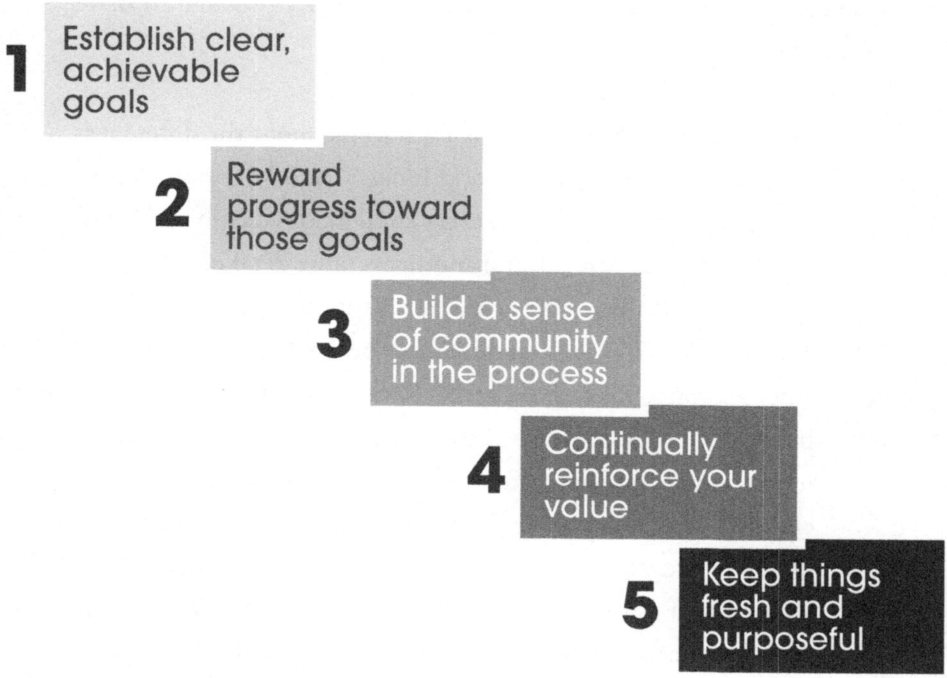

1. Establish Clear, Achievable Goals

Recall from Chapter 1 that an individual's expectation of their own success in the short- and long-term occupies a primary place in their motivation. When a member of your audience first comes across your message, they'll want to know how they can help, what's in it for them, and how likely they are to receive a reward. Once you convert them, these needs don't go away, so the ways in which you communicate your organization's goals—and your convert's contribution to them—will be critical to maintaining engagement over time.

What does success look like for your initiative? Are you trying to commercialize a new technology? Plant more trees? Clean the local water supply? From your customer's perspective, it's important that you are very specific regarding your goal. And by specific, I mean SMART.

SMART Goals

The SMART acronym was originally proposed in the early 1980s to help organizations determine if their objectives were clear enough to drive meaningful action. The acronym stands for:

- **Specific:** Be as detailed as possible. Think about the differences between "we want to end world hunger" and "we want to provide three free meals a day to every child in Philadelphia." One of them is extremely broad, and another is quite detailed. The more specific you are, the more achievable your goal will be.
- **Measurable:** Choose a goal that can be tracked, so you can see whether you're making progress. To continue the hunger example, measurements of world hunger certainly exist, but they're much harder to quantify at a detailed level than the number of children in school in a particular city, and how many meals those children received.
- **Achievable:** A single individual will have a hard time thinking they can make a dent in global hunger, but they can certainly

donate canned goods or volunteer to serve meals one day a month in their city. While you might feel pressure to set an audacious goal, it's more engaging and motivating to keep your goals realistic and achievable within your available time and resources.

- **Realistic:** If challenges were easy, they'd already be solved. Your challenge likely faces some combination of a lack of resources, technical or scientific limitations, economic factors, political factors, or other issues. When you're setting your goals, don't pretend those factors don't exist. Instead, focus on what's possible based on your organization's maturity, resources, and level of influence. If you're a new organization with a handful of volunteers and staff, maybe you start with just serving enough meals in schools to cover one month out of the year, and then work your way up to solving world hunger.
- **Timely:** Nothing lasts forever, particularly an audience's attention. Setting a time-bound objective helps focus effort, reduce volunteer fatigue, and provide an achievable "end point" you can use to measure progress.

Are Mission and Vision Statements Clear, Achievable Goals?

If you're familiar with brand theory, you likely know about two of the more common foundational components: mission and vision statements.

- A **mission statement** tells your audience why you're in business in the first place. It's another way of expressing your value proposition, and should include a tactical focus on the near term.
- **Vision statements**, on the other hand, are aspirational. They declare what impact your organization would like to make in the future, and often focus beyond just your audience's needs.

I'd love to tell you that all of the work marketing strategists and brand theorists put into wordsmithing their mission and vision statements is carefully pored over by every customer, but the vast majority of people makes purchases without ever knowing the mission or vision statement of the products and solutions we choose.

For example, did you know this was Coca-Cola's vision statement? "Our vision is to craft the brands and choice of drinks that people love, to refresh them in body & spirit. And done in ways that create a more sustainable business and better shared future that makes a difference in people's lives, communities, and our planet."[6]

You probably didn't. If you bought a Coke recently, it was likely for the taste, cost, or convenience (there we go with value proposition theory again).

Mission and vision statements tend to target a different audience than your typical customer. They serve as internal tools to motivate and focus employees' decision-making, and as external statements to help align stakeholders who can create collective action. Both of these elements can be critical for cause marketers.

Let's take a look at a few mission statements to see what we mean:

Green America

Mission statement: *"Green America harnesses economic power—the strength of consumers, investors, businesses, and the marketplace—to create a socially just and environmentally sustainable society."*

This mission statement tells you exactly what Green America wants to accomplish, but at the same time it's still quite lofty. Harnessing economic power is a hard thing for an individual to accomplish, and you don't see many of the SMART elements we discussed above.

Bombas

Mission statement: *"Our mission since day one has been to help those experiencing homelessness. That's why for every item you purchase, we donate an item on your behalf."*

On the more tactical side, Bombas has an extremely simple mission—the donation of clothing to those in need. This mission is clear and extremely achievable. It's not promising the world, just telling you exactly where the company's focus is and what it will do as a socially conscious business.

Once you've clearly stated your goals, it would be nice if you could snap your fingers and reach them. But progress takes time, and each day that passes puts your audience engagement at risk. That's why you need to keep them invested in your progress as well.

2. Reward Progress Toward Those Goals

We are creatures not of habit, but of dopamine, which is a chemical our brains release in anticipation of receiving a reward. Psychologists break down these rewards into two types:

- **Internal rewards:** Those that our senses deem pleasurable on their own, such as dessert, or a hot shower, or a good nap.
- **External (or conditioned) rewards:** Those we are conditioned to anticipate through actions and praise from authorities such as our parents, teachers, managers, and societal leaders. Examples here would be trophies for winning a competition, a bonus for doing a good job at work, and so on.

What does the dopamine-driven reward cycle look like in reality?

I once read a very interesting anonymous exposé from a research chemist in the snack food industry. Based on research that food can be addictive,[7] his team had been assigned to test a new flavor profile by comparing brain scans of taste testers against the scans of heroin addicts, in order to try and mimic similar states of excitement and dopamine levels in the brain. The end goal, of course, was to develop a product that became as (legally) addictive as possible in the hope that the customer's craving would never let them choose an alternative.

If only we could all be so lucky with our causes.

We're certainly not trying to get our audience addicted to anything other than good, clean living, but we are trying to create a similar feedback loop where our audience becomes conditioned to seek a reward from us so they keep returning. To solve this challenge and keep their audiences engaged, many organizations use a common tactic called "gamification" when structuring their reward program.

Would You Like to Play a Game?

The concept of gamification has entered the motivational theory lexicon over the last thirty-plus years thanks to the massive success of video games, which focus on a recurring cycle of immediate engagement and near-term reward. Video games strive to provide a player with what's known as a "power fantasy"—the ability to take control of a compelling situation and level up enough to overcome all obstacles. When the game ends, of course, you share your achievement success with your friends, and start a new game.

This cycle maps closely to the individual motivational theory psychologists call **self-determination theory** (SDT). SDT posits that individuals have three basic psychological needs that must be satisfied for motivation to exist:[8]

1. **Autonomy:** the ability to control one's own life and exercise free will
2. **Competence (or Mastery):** the desire to control an outcome through our own skill
3. **Relatedness (or Relationships):** the experience of interacting and connecting with others

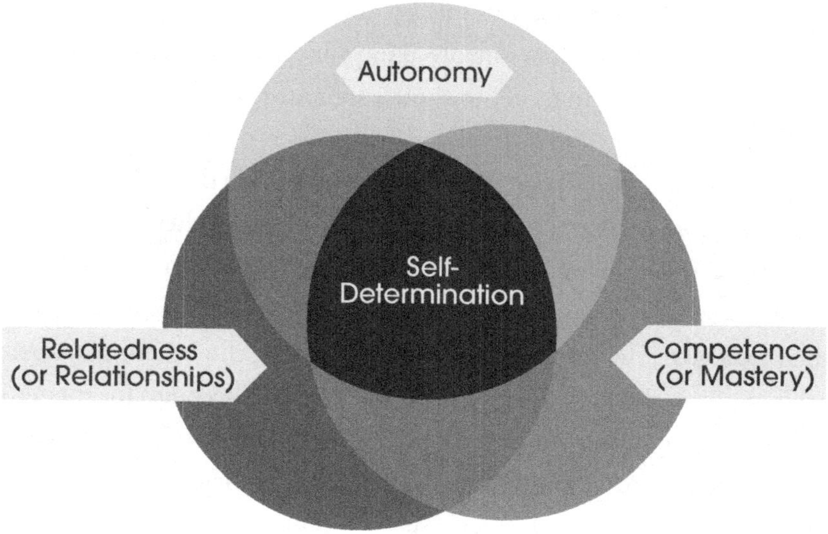

On the surface, these concepts might seem a bit too academic for a cause marketer. But if you think about them as stages of a game that's trying to move a player through various levels, you can see many similarities to an audience journey, making these needs key to reducing churn and keeping your converted audience members engaged.

Autonomy

Remember that humans are motivated by the expectation of success. If you're concerned about a particular cause, nothing can be more disheartening than feeling like you don't make a difference. The individuals who join your cause want to see that they are taking back some level of control over their pain point, so to keep them engaged you'll want to continually demonstrate what success looks like.

There are a number of ways to do this:

- Emphasize individual power and control in your messaging
- Show successful examples from your cause, and the factors that led to that success

- Communicate progress toward milestones, and what comes next
- Highlight big names involved in your cause (partners, sponsors, politicians, and more) to show a sphere of control

It's critical to show your audience how they made these changes happen. The more autonomy your audience derives from their efforts with your cause, the more tightly they'll bind their identities to that cause.

You can also give your audience autonomy by letting them choose their own goals (within reason). Individuals value choice, but paradoxically, the more options you give them the harder it becomes for them to choose one.[9] So plan your new convert's initial journey by giving them a small set of easy-to-accomplish items that can give them a quick win and deliver immediate value through a sense of achievement.

You can find a good example of this approach in LinkedIn's sign-up process. Upon registration, the guide provides a step-by-step walk-through of the different fields LinkedIn wants you to complete, alongside a completion percentage bar that dangles like a carrot, urging you to get to 100.

Competence

Self-doubt seems to be built into human nature. As a result, we seek validation of our competence from third parties and external sources. Entering competitions, asking for reviews, getting our friends' feedback, and seeking second opinions are all examples of this behavior.

Your organization and its endorsement can play that same role. Methods to encourage and grow your audience's sense of competence can include:

- Certifications and validations
- Awards and recognition for higher participation levels (hours volunteered, donations raised, etc.)

- Membership or service tiers that offer exclusive rewards and access
- Tools like badges, leaderboards, and performance graphs[10]

Let's take a look at how one organization uses gamification to keep its volunteers engaged through a competence-focused approach:

Points for Blood: How the Red Cross Gamifies Volunteering

You're likely familiar with the Red Cross's blood donation drives. Did you know that, just like airline miles on a credit card, you can get points for donating blood? The Red Cross unveiled a blood donor reward program at the beginning of 2025 that offers 100 points for each donation, with points able to be redeemed for gifts like jackets, tumblers, and more.[11]

While we might not think these small tokens matter much, their enduring popularity is a sign that do-gooders like to show off just like anyone else, and that they are attracted to these kinds of offers and incentives.

Suggestions for Reward Delivery

As you build your reward program, the notes below may help:

- **Speed matters:** In today's era of instant gratification, it's important to give rewards for task completion quickly and consistently. Doing so improves trust and makes your audience more likely to continue their efforts.
- **Laddering:** Make sure you provide higher rewards and greater recognition for those who spend more time with your cause. This allows your most dedicated evangelists to feel special.

- **Simplicity matters:** You'll see more traction if you keep your tasks quick and easy. Remember, you're asking for people to volunteer their time, and the perceived cost of that time needs to match the reward. If you do have complexity, say for a complicated task, build it slowly by giving your audience quick wins first before progressing toward bigger challenges.
- **Give public recognition:** Have you heard of the network effect? It means that the value of something depends on the number of individuals involved who value that item, activity, or reward. It also means that the more people hear about something, the more likely they are to become interested in it and assign it a value. So the more you can publicly recognize your audience, the better and easier it will be to find more leaders.
- **Make things fun:** A big component of the success of donation drives like the Ice Bucket Challenge and Movember is the fun involved. People are happy to volunteer their time if they enjoy the experience and if it helps put others in a good mood.

3. Build a Sense of Community in the Process

Relatedness

Self-determination theory's third component, relatedness, states that human motivation comes from our innate need to form community and feel a sense of belonging. It's likely that this need evolved hundreds of thousands of years ago, when we were just tribes of hairless apes who huddled together to survive in a world full of lions and tigers and bears. But that need still exists today.

In fact, our need for community has grown so acute that numerous studies have shown that we are experiencing a "crisis of belonging," and the U.S. Surgeon General has even issued a warning about the dangers of loneliness.[12]

What better solution can we offer than uniting around a positive cause?

Studies show that sharing meaningful stories with teammates can improve social relatedness and participation.[13] As a cause marketer, you'll want to think about how you can build community starting from your very first interaction with your audience. You'll want them to feel that bond of common purpose, the sense that they're part of a larger whole.

Great communities encourage their members to share experiences, be heard, and feel validated through any number of online and in-person community activities, including:

- **A warm initial greeting:** Your ideal customer interaction begins with a warm welcome. Volunteer ambassadors, personalized outreach, event greeters, and anything else you can think of to make your new converts feel welcome will help you cement the social connection between your cause and your new volunteers.
- **Shared signals and rituals:** For thousands of years, organizations have been using secret handshakes, code words, rituals, and imagery to affirm their sense of belonging. Today, those totems might look like hashtags, avatar icons, and bumper stickers, but the same rule still applies.
- **Strong internal communications:** When planning your newsletters and social media, the more you can feature stories from your community, the more its members will feel they can share their own stories and be celebrated (hopefully with a healthy dose of peer pressure to push others to do something shareable).
- **In-person events:** Charity walks and runs, park cleanups, beautification and planting projects, fundraisers, competitions, rallies, and galas are all excellent ways to grow a community. And while in-person events are often the most expensive and logistically complex, they often go the furthest in creating a sense of community.

- **Joint problem solving:** A former colleague was fond of the saying "nothing pulls a team together like putting them in a room and asking them to solve a problem." His philosophy was that setting a goal shifts a group into collaborative gear and gives them something to achieve, which can help build a sense of community stemming from the collective accomplishment. You can achieve the same effect by establishing committees, inviting solution submissions, and holding contests.

Example: The Kidney Walk

If you know anyone with kidney disease, you've likely heard of the National Kidney Foundation (NKF). NKF raises money for a number of kidney-related programs, including supporting the kidney donor registry, providing education for kidney clinicians, and educating patients and their families about treatment options.

One of their biggest fundraising activities is the Kidney Walk, where a local organizer puts together a walk and invites team captains to sign up and create teams. The teams then recruit donors to support their walk. NKF holds nearly 100 walks a year, with more than 75,000 individuals signing up to fundraise and participate. Each event has a significant digital and press presence, which contributes to the strong sense of community felt by participants.

4. Continually Reinforce Your Value

Did you know that doing good can generate a positive feedback loop? Researchers have found that rewarding social innovation leads to more social entrepreneurship behavior,[14] which bodes well for your efforts to keep your audience engaged. You just need to make sure your audience feels that continual reward over time.

This is a more significant challenge than it might seem, because self-determination theory does have some limits. Constantly dangling carrots in front of your audience can fatigue their dopamine response, and does not work as well when the intended results are not as tangible or trackable as a pint of blood. You will need to work harder to keep your audience engaged after their initial excitement has worn off and the size of the mountain you're asking them to climb becomes more apparent (more on this in Chapter 7).

Expectancy–value theory (EVT) provides a great approach to help you think about how to deliver continuous value over longer time frames. EVT focuses on two primary factors influencing human motivation: [15]

1. **Expectancy:** The strength of an individual's belief that their effort will lead to success, in either the short or long term. This metric can be thought of as an individual's self-assessment of their own confidence. Do they have the experience, skill, and external validation to feel that they can achieve what is asked or required of them?
2. **Value:** The importance an individual places on the work required to receive the potential reward. An individual may build their value assessment from a number of different components depending on the type of decision, including:
    - Enjoyment
    - Utility
    - Capacity
    - Cost

    For example, a busy person who ignores a coworker's request to join a fundraising event may have decided that they do not have the time to devote to an activity at the moment, but later on they may be interested in watching a funny video on the same topic because they are looking for a way to relax and are placing more value on being entertained.

EVT believes human decision-making criteria is extremely dynamic: as we are presented with new information and choices on a daily basis, we constantly revise our personal expectancy and value calculations due to our environment and the feedback we've received.

An individual operating within a familiar environment, such as an industry in which they have work experience, will have much greater confidence in their potential success than someone starting a new career in a highly technical industry with a steep learning curve. Cultural factors can also affect EVT. Different cultures place different societal values on criteria such as individual independence and acceptance of failure, which in turn may change the weighting of the two primary values.

And while we can add weighting to the expectancy value model in order to compensate for those criteria, your audience's core choice will always boil down to the simple question of "Why do I want to do this?"

If social innovation is regularly rewarded in the system you are creating, an individual will have their answer.

Let's take a look at one example of an EVT-based approach in action.

Case Study: How Microsoft Takes Carbon Credits One Step Further

One of the biggest challenges humanity faces is the environmental stress brought on by climate change. And yet, many of the changes needed seem to be massively controversial or ignored. EVT might provide a way around this logjam.

As an example, let's look at climate change and carbon credits. It can be very easy to tune out the dire warnings about increasing global temperatures, because it's not clear exactly how an individual's efforts can make a difference. Plenty of travel sites, for example, will offer carbon offset purchases for a few additional dollars, but compared to corporate carbon expenditures, those purchases feel like a drop in the bucket due to the low expectancy of success.

At the corporate level, the carbon offset market would have seen two straight years of declines in 2022 and 2023 if not for a surge in December purchases that was likely motivated by the need to lower tax burdens.[16] Many corporate purchasers now view offsets as greenwashing or even fraudulent due to a number of scandals about ineffective oversight of the offset programs.[17] And when a company is spending money largely for a public relations benefit, it can't afford to be involved in a scandal.

So how does one generate an expectation of success and value in this environment? Enter Microsoft.

In 2009, Microsoft began a series of commitments and investments to reduce its carbon footprint that included an internal carbon tax, levied on each business unit by the corporate entity, of at least $15 per metric ton of carbon generated. Among other efforts, Microsoft's success has led the company to be able to confidently claim it will be carbon negative by 2030.[18, 19]

Why has Microsoft succeeded where other companies have failed? They focused on value and expectancy.

The first priority listed in Microsoft's carbon fee increase announcement was a move toward sustainable facilities and data centers. If you're not familiar with the enormous water and energy requirements of a modern data center, all you really need to know is that, at the time I'm writing this book, Amazon, Microsoft, and OpenAI are all considering operating their own nuclear power plants to power their data centers.

So for Microsoft, the value of a carbon tax isn't really in the carbon itself, it's a way to help the company improve its operating costs and margins by reducing a significant expense over time. And as Microsoft has progressed in this space, it has built an expectancy of success. The company has increased its internal carbon tax several times, while also moving up its carbon neutral time horizon.

While Microsoft's efforts are self-serving, they also illustrate the power of the expectancy value theory. If you are able to establish a powerful value and track your expectations of success, you can move mountains. Or smash atoms.

But Microsoft's EVT approach isn't the only way organizations can reinforce value over time.

Investment and Exchange Theories:

If you think of the value you deliver to your audience from the perspective of a return on their investment, you can look to investment theory for ways to keep your audience engaged and satisfied. Investment theories parallel many of the other motivational theories we've discussed so far, and tend to fall into two camps:

- **Personal investment theory**: This states that people invest their time and effort in activities that align with their personal goals, interests, and values in a given context. This theory echoes SDT's position that individuals seek achievement and a sense of autonomy, but factors in external conditions. For example, a student is motivated to perform well if they are interested in the subject matter (a personal alignment) and come from a family that places strong emphasis on academic performance (an external factor).
- **Social investment and exchange theories:** The opposite end of the spectrum places heavier weight on external factors, positing that individuals' motivations and investments change over time as they seek to occupy different roles in society.[20] As a result, individuals become motivated to make social investments such as volunteering or entering local politics based on their expected return for the social position they seek to occupy. If they perceive their social reward to be bigger than the cost required to receive the reward, they will act.

Regardless of which theory you subscribe to, they provide a clear guide for your audience's expected return on investment. If your audience research from Chapter 2 reveals that you're working with more individually motivated people, you'll want to slant your communications and rewards toward the individual achievement celebrations that comprise gamification's core.

On the other hand, if your participants are drawn to the idea of making a larger impact outside themselves, you'll want to emphasize big-picture progress. That might include demonstrating positive social returns by mentioning increasing involvement from notable people and organizations that your cause has impacted.

To sum up how you can reinforce your cause's value and purpose, first identify exactly what your audience values through your market research, and then make sure to deliver and communicate that value as early and often as possible.

5. Keep Things Fresh

If game theory perfectly described the human mind, we'd all be locked in our rooms playing games for the rest of our lives. But we evolve, grow bored, and want something new.

In my experience, people tend to be attracted to novel tasks and put their heaviest effort into their first attempts, with the dopamine rush of something new adding a sense of excitement that later repetitions will never quite match.[21] Once we're satisfied, or we feel we've learned all we can, we move on.

Sociologist George Homans's social exchange theory provides some insight into the reasons behind this fatigue. Homans based his theory of human decision-making on an economic model of costs and rewards as determined by society, with three "propositions" that affect our decisions:

1. **Success:** When someone finds they are rewarded for their actions, they tend to repeat the action.
2. **Stimulus:** The more often a particular stimulus has resulted in a reward in the past, the more likely it is that a person will respond to it.

3. **Deprivation-satiation:** The more often a person has received a particular reward in the recent past, the less valuable any further unit of that reward becomes.[22]

The last point is most salient for us—tactics like gamification can only take audience engagement so far, because people will eventually grow tired of the rewards we have to offer. As we've just discussed, you can extend the engagement cycle by focusing on longer-term value delivery, but you'll still be fighting against your audience's satiation.

So how can you keep things fresh? You can try a number of ideas:

- **Change team roles:** Sometimes, people just need a fresh perspective to maintain interest.
- **Adjust your focus:** New rewards, different goals, or a change in priorities can help rekindle interest and excitement.
- **Refresh your creative:** Adjusting your message, outreach tactics, or creative assets can help refresh your efforts.
- **Introduce co-creation:** Inviting your audience to share their perspective regarding your efforts can bring new ideas to the table and reinvigorate a campaign.

If you believe Homans's theory, these tactics will also fall victim to ebbs and flows of enthusiasm. So how can you insulate your audience against this inevitable erosion of interest?

The best way to keep them invested is with purpose.

You Can't Spell Cause Without "P"

One of the big gaps that many of the motivational models we've discussed have when it comes to cause marketing is the "Big P:" purpose.

You likely became attached to your cause because you felt the desire either to do whatever g ood you could through meaningful work, or to be part of something greater in order to make an impact. And you are not alone.

No less an authority on our wants and needs than Google has spent long years studying human needs in order to improve its team-building through what it called "Project Aristotle." The study found that two of the most important aspects to a successful team were:

- **Meaning:** finding purpose in a group's work
- **Impact:** seeing the group's work drive change and improvement[23]

We've seen glimmers of purpose-driven motivation throughout this book, but have stayed largely focused on tapping into intrinsic, internal motivational factors in order to generate action and deliver the value required to remain in business. Yet the people who attach themselves to your cause are also looking for more.

Returning to our discussion of brand evangelists earlier in this chapter, would you be at all surprised to know that some people take their brand associations so far they actually build a portion of their identity around the brand?[24]

The best way to ensure you are keeping your audience satisfied and delivering value is for your cause to give their lives a real sense of purpose.

How does this work? Let's examine the RAMP model for an explanation.

The RAMP model adds a fourth element to self-determination theory's concepts of relatedness, autonomy, and mastery (its version of competence): **purpose.**

Defined as an understanding that our actions will support an ultimate objective that has personal meaning to us, purpose underscores Google's team-building findings and speaks to the heart of what your cause is really trying to deliver.

If you can link your cause tightly to your audience's identity, you'll always be able to keep the experience fresh by giving them the ability to create new versions of your solution. That allows your audience to strike out on their own journey under your banner, while promoting you along the way.

FINAL THOUGHTS: TO THE HEAVENS

By now, you've hopefully generated an army of engaged supporters ready to tackle any challenge for your cause. Let's conclude with a few notes to make sure your evangelists keep on singing:

- **Your audience must trust that you will do what you promise.** Going back to your value proposition, the promise you make to your target audience in any of those categories must be ironclad. The last thing you want is for someone to recommend you to a friend, only for that friend to have a different, less valuable experience. It's critical to keep your brand promise at all times.[25]
- **Deliver a best-in-class experience.** The more your target audience believes their experience sets them apart from others (or other solutions), the more likely they will be to share it widely. Providing unique experiences, access, or other opportunities that an individual would not have been able to achieve on their own can help create evangelists.
- **Tell emotional stories.** Remember the power of emotion? You'll want to use that power to generate a feeling within your audience. It might be something like belonging, or hope, or excitement. But you're trying to create and harness that emotion at scale in order to get people talking about you.
- **Listen and respond to feedback.** Finally, the most powerful tool you have is the ability to listen and respond to ideas and suggestions from your target audience. Individuals who participate in the creation and evolution of something have a vested interest in seeing it succeed, and they love to share their success with others who can help them.

We've come a long way, but our work still isn't done. In the next chapter, we'll examine the roadblocks you might encounter—and how to overcome them in order to keep growing your impact.

7

Driving Change at Scale

LEADING THE BLIND

Change is hard. On an individual level, every one of us has habits we struggle to break, improvements we never get around to making, or challenges we lack the resources to solve. In fact, 45 percent of us fail our New Year's resolutions every year.[1] When we take our cause to others, the going gets even tougher. Not everyone understands what we're trying to accomplish, or agrees with our goals, or even acknowledges the problem we see. And thanks to this resistance, any number of societal ills fester.

But you didn't make it this far because you're afraid of a challenge.

At this point, your solution has established a toehold in the market. You've got some of your audience singing your praises, and your cause is growing to the point where you can risk taking some bigger swings at larger chunks of the market. And I have good news for you: conquering resistance to change might not be as hard as you'd think.

We may think that beliefs are very strongly held and impossible to change, but research does not bear out this assumption. Thanks to a phenomenon known as **choice blindness,** humans have been proven to be quite susceptible to alternate versions and explanations for the choices we've made. It's even possible to convince someone that they've made a choice they really didn't. The majority of research participants will even go so far as defending their (false) choice to researchers.[2]

Researchers have demonstrated that choice blindness exists in a number of subject areas, including political messaging.[3] The ubiquity of this phenomenon indicates just how quickly social pressure created by an in-group (in this case the researchers) can shift people's beliefs. Of course, your audience isn't living their lives in a research laboratory where you can directly manipulate their choices. But their beliefs are much more malleable than you might think.

This chapter will examine communication approaches designed to change people's minds at scale. We're going to start by examining the three core reasons people resist change: **ignorance, fear,** and **inertia.** Along the way, we'll review communications strategies to overcome this resistance:

- Education and trust
- Emotional communications
- Habit-breaking
- Co-creation
- Power building

This might sound like a tall order. But don't worry, we're going to start with a ladder.

CLIMBING THE LADDER OF INFLUENCE

Organizational psychologist Chris Argyris has developed a helpful change management concept called the "ladder of influence," which frames our decision-making process as a continuous seven-step cycle of making choices based on inputs and processing the results of those inputs to inform future decisions. The seven steps are:

1. **Observed experience (aka "Reality").** At the first step, we process what we see and experience in the world around us. While we like to consider our received information to be factual and objective, in truth many of us choose to recollect events in ways that are more favorable to our own psyches (for example, in the choice blindness experiments). Which leads us to step 2.
2. **Filtered/selected reality.** Remember the goldfish from Chapter 4? Our minds constantly and automatically filter the massive amount of information our senses receive based on our beliefs and prior experiences, which means we are hard-wired to ignore contrary information. When you try to generate awareness, you're chipping away at the filtered reality of your audience.
3. **Meaning/interpretation.** Once we allow information to reach us, we then go to work interpreting and assigning meaning to what we've seen. If we witnessed an accident, whose fault was it, and why? Why did our team lose the game? The effort we spend searching for meaning can intensify when we address actions outside of our control.
4. **Assumptions.** This step is where we check our mental work. We all have preexisting assumptions about how events should go—the type of service we should expect at a restaurant, or how we'll be greeted in a meeting, for example. But these assumptions are malleable. At this stage, we're matching our assumptions against what we've observed to see if our assumptions still hold true or if we need to change our interpretation.
5. **Conclusions.** At the fifth step of the influence ladder, we're ready to decide. We've come up with an explanation of what we've experienced based on the data we have in front of us, and we're firming up our position. Which leads to . . .
6. **Beliefs.** We build beliefs based on repeated experiences that support our conclusions. These beliefs may concern other people, the world around us, product quality, our own

competency, or anything else. Our belief consists of our current emotional truth about a particular subject, as best we can construct it.

7. **Actions.** At the final rung of the influence ladder, we find ourselves taking action based on our beliefs. The results of that action then provide us with our next set of observed experiences, and we start the process all over again.

The influence ladder is a tool that helps us imagine all the points of potential change resistance that occur in an individual's mind and understand how to soothe that resistance.

WHY DO WE RESIST?

When we reviewed the decision funnel, we looked at ways to move your audience toward a decision, but we didn't cover all the points of friction that can slow or stop their journey. This resistance may come from any number of sources, but the motivational theories we've studied so far tend to group that resistance into three core causes:

- Ignorance
- Fear
- Inertia

These groupings can manifest in conscious or unconscious ways, and present at both the individual and societal levels. We'll examine each in detail below.

Resistance Factor 1: Ignorance

For our purposes, let's define ignorance as a situation where someone in your audience doesn't know the scale or scope of your challenge and resists efforts to address the problem until they receive further information. You'll typically encounter ignorance in two forms: lack of awareness and cognitive bias.

Lack of Awareness

Chapter 4 detailed the many challenges you'll experience generating awareness of your issue. An additional factor is that when it comes to ignorance, many people willfully choose the bliss that comes with it.

In an environment of information overload that simultaneously tries to use emotions and outrage to get us to care about any number of issues, many people turn to ignorance as a mental defense mechanism. This phenomenon, known as **media fatigue,** arises from the constant blizzard of demands for our attention from the media we consume and the emotional exhaustion these demands generate.[4] It is very common for individuals experiencing these issues to withdraw from media consumption and put their heads firmly in the sand to preserve their own sanity.

I can't really say that I blame them, either.

But in spite of the dual threat of media saturation and media fatigue, ignorance in many ways is the easiest source of resistance to counter. Much of what we've discussed in this book so far involves delivering information, so we won't revisit it here. But in summary, to address ignorance, you'll need to focus on education:

1. Make your audience aware of the challenge—capture their attention through whatever means necessary (Chapter 4).
2. Show them how they'll benefit from solving the challenge, ideally using your solution.
3. Incentivize them to take action.
4. Demonstrate the value they receive from their action as early and often as possible.

Cognitive Bias

Remember that our minds don't really want to think more than they have to, so we tend to rely on our previous experience and assumptions to guide our actions rather than gathering and processing new information. This phenomenon is a type of cognitive bias that discourages us from seeking out new knowledge, and it affects all of us.

If you've ever found yourself turning back to your favorite music channel rather than seeking something new, or taking the familiar route home instead of following someone else's suggestion, you've experienced the same bias. On a societal level, the older we get, the less inclined most of us are to try new things.

But cognitive bias, too, can be countered.

Research has shown that "approach-oriented" techniques can help counter bias-driven ignorance by encouraging an individual to try something new and providing support as they do so.[5] Rather than emphasizing avoidance (e.g. "Don't buy a plastic water bottle"), your goal should be to provide an alternative and encourage its trial ("Would you like a free reusable water bottle? You can fill it at the water fountain").

Depending on how deeply the bias you're combatting is seated, you may need to adopt a series of approach tactics that build up your audience's comfort. For example, if you are trying to improve police-citizen relations within a community that demonstrates significant distrust of authority, you may need to first encourage a few individuals to participate in small actions like ride-alongs or community events before working up to bigger objectives.

Fighting Ignorance through Education and Trust

Education is your best tool to fight ignorance. When focusing on education as a change driver, your goal is to become a trusted source of information for your audience. While the approaches to growing awareness we've discussed in Chapters 3 and 4 will help get your educational process started, you'll want to continue the conversation with your audience through a number of other channels in order to build trust. These can include:

- Communicating through already-trusted channels, such as influencers or public relations
- Working through social networks to leverage peers
- Establishing yourself as an expert in the field
- Inviting your audience to participate in solution building
- Aligning with academic, government, or corporate sources to demonstrate trust

Depending on your trust-building strategies, you may be able to use a participatory approach in your communications. Think about an effort to support schoolchildren that leverages the PTA and school board networks as well as educators to have all three groups push the same message. If you can get these groups to co-create and agree on the message, they'll be much more likely to help with the communications due to the shared sense of ownership you've created.

It will also be important to do what you say you will. Nothing destroys trust faster than a failed promise to your audience.

Resistance Factor 2: Fear

We've already learned that fear is one of the most powerful human motivational emotions, and it plays a strong role in preventing action as well. Recent research posits that habit formation and stickiness occurs in the same brain structures that generate our emotional neurotransmitters, which means the thought of changing a habit may generate literal fear.[9]

THE IMPORTANCE OF EMPATHY IN BUILDING TRUST

One of the keys to changing someone's mind is to not worry about changing their mind at all. Instead, focus on building a relationship and understanding your target's point of view. This approach relies on our social nature—we are more likely to listen to someone who's demonstrated their concern and respect for us over time, versus someone who immediately tells us we're wrong without any precursor and puts us on the defensive.

We've all been in situations where we haven't been in a mindset to listen. And in those situations, starting with attacking language like "you need to," etc., is a quick way to lose your audience.

But those individuals who slow down, build connections, and establish rapport are much more likely to have their own views heard when the time comes. As the saying goes, seek first to understand, then to be understood.

Some of the most successful interrogators of World War II were not torturers, but people who chose to treat their prisoners well while asking them questions. The German Hanns Scharff established a method of relationship building backed by selective truth-telling to encourage his prisoners to volunteer information,[6] while the British went so far as to create a separate luxury prison for captured senior German officers, giving them gifts like shopping trips to Harrod's and visits from royalty to loosen their lips.[7]

Another example of relationship building is Daryl Davis, a black musician from Chicago who has reportedly convinced hundreds of members of the KKK to abandon their activities by sitting down with them for dinner and conversation.[8]

Once the relationship is established, you have a level of trust that you can use to further your message.

So your audience's choice to change must overcome significant, deep-seated concerns of which they likely aren't even consciously aware.

These deep-seated fears can be grouped into four rough categories:

The Unknown

When you take immediate survival-related fears out of the equation—falling, starving, spiders, etc.—the cause of most fear boils down to the unknown. The human brain is wired to seek predictability and stability,[10] making any deviation from the norm potentially threatening. This fear of the unknown likely reflects an innate survival instinct. We don't know what will happen if we act, but we know we're "safe" in the moment and will stay that way if we simply . . . don't act. Our minds seek safety in what we know.[11]

When you're asking someone to join your cause, understand that you may be asking them to step out onto a psychological limb that's too shaky for their brain's wiring.

Social Fears

What do we do when we're afraid? We cling to each other for safety in numbers. As social animals who evolved with few innate physical means to defend ourselves, we had to band together to survive. As a result, we are constantly evaluating our own social position and anything that might cause us to lose face or rank in our larger group. These social fears are some of the strongest we deal with on a daily basis.

To lessen our social anxiety, we subconsciously identify the rules of the in-group and act accordingly. As a result, nothing is more rewarding to us than seeing a positive, affirming message about our chosen group—our football team won, our volunteer group was recognized for its generosity, etc. These kinds of affirmations mean our identity is "right." And to avoid cognitive dissonance, we must preserve the rightness of that group for our own psychological safety.

When you see a group of people whose actions seem irrational or impervious to facts and data, they are acting out of social fear. They are responding at an emotional level and not a "rational" level, as an independent observer would perceive it, so their justifications for their own behavior don't need to make sense. All they need to do is soothe the cognitive dissonance that occurs when presented with threatening information.

These in-groups will cling to their positions in spite of evidence to the contrary because they are responding to social cues from those around them, not factual evidence. To accept that a group has been wrong would signal that their identity itself is flawed, and the psychological fear that results from this scenario can be strong enough to lead someone to reject all evidence to the contrary.

We are all guilty of this behavior, whether in an argument with a partner, a disagreement at work, or any number of other situations. And the reality is that fact-based arguments will not change the mind of anyone predisposed against your idea. You must communicate on an emotional level to address the underlying social fears.

Lack of Control

The world is a big, chaotic place over which we have a terrifyingly small level of control. Weather, disease, car accidents, asteroids, and earthquakes could all strike at any moment, and that chaotic randomness can cause fear. Each year, Chapman University does a Survey of American Fears, and issues that lie outside of our individual control—such as government corruption, economic collapse, war, and illness—regularly top the list.[12]

The COVID-19 pandemic provides an excellent example of this kind of fear-driven behavior. When the virus forced the world to radically alter how it operated in order to slow the disease's spread, people transferred their fears over a lack of control to behavior that they could control. Wearing a mask was akin to acknowledging how serious the disease was, and how anyone could get it. That fear struck directly against the belief that "it won't happen to me" or "I'm stronger than the virus", and generated what's called **psychological reactance,** which is when someone does the opposite of what is requested in order to soothe a perceived lack of control.[13] The end result for COVID-19 was that a vocal minority chose to go maskless and forgo or protest the vaccines.

To soothe issues of control, you can adopt a co-creation approach that gives your audience ownership of their choices and paths.

Economic Fears

We've all had worries about our jobs, the economy, or the price of groceries. And with so many of us incorporating our livelihood into our personal identity, a threat to our job becomes a threat to our sense of self. These economic fears combine the unknown and a lack of control into a survival threat: how will we support ourselves if the bottom falls out?

These fears also apply to your individual audience and the organizations and systems you seek to change.

Remember how we started this book with a company's decision to save a few pennies on cups? While personal altruism may or may not exist, organizational altruism definitely does not.

Organizational decision-makers don't live in daily fear, but they do base their primary decision criteria on the perceived harm their organization might face if a change occurs. From this viewpoint, a loss of market share will lead to lower revenues, which will lead to lower compensation, which will lead to some level of personal and possibly professional injury that those individuals would prefer to avoid. And the greater the challenge to that organization's survival, the harder the organization will fight against your change.

As an example, look at plastic manufacturers' current efforts to lobby for reduced recycling requirements and labeling.[14] Billions of dollars and thousands of jobs are on the line if the system of plastics usage in the US changes. That entire ecosystem will fight tooth and nail against any proposed change until compelled by a more powerful force, regardless of the greater societal good.

We've seen the same pattern repeat for the tobacco industry, the oil industry, and so many others. The solution to addressing economic-based fears is to capture power.

Fighting Fear

Emotional Approaches

The emotional grip fear holds over your audience is best countered with an emotional message. Research has shown that changing someone's mind via media alone requires you to be three times more persuasive than the typical media message,[15] which means your communications will need to pack an even stronger emotional punch. The question is, which emotional chord should you strike?

Recall that while both negative and positive messages generate results, positive emotional content ultimately wins over time. So you may want to have a one-two punch of emotional content prepared, with your jab being the repeated drumbeat of fear to prime your audience, and your uppercut being a more comforting, welcoming message to ease concern and provide emotional support.

Enthusiasm

Research shows that there's no more positive motivator than enthusiasm.[16] We tend to mirror and mimic others, so one of the most powerful ways to change someone's emotional state is to expose them to others who espouse the positives of the change you'd like to see. This can be done on an individual, person-to-person level through your team, volunteers, and brand evangelists. At scale, you should look to channels like these:

- Traditional media
- Social media
- Rallies and events
- Signs and out-of-home advertising

- Networking and sponsorship through third parties (interest groups, associations, etc.)
- Engaging with community leaders

Your goal when adopting an enthusiasm campaign is simply to show that your audience's peers share a certain value set and are acting in a certain way, then give your audience members the chance to experience it for themselves. The more passion and excitement you and your evangelists bring to the cause, the more powerful your message will become.

Enthusiasm campaigns carry risks: the excitement of the new is ephemeral, and people who start off energized by a cause may drift away as the less glamorous parts of the work emerge. Manufactured enthusiasm, such as paid influencer campaigns, also often rarely lasts due to the competitiveness and short attention span of the consumer market.

But you can also demonstrate enthusiasm through an unflagging commitment to your cause. The more positive, affirming messages you provide over a long period of time, the better chance your audience will have of adopting your enthusiasm.

Shame

While showering your audience with enthusiasm can be effective, you may not want to shy away from low blows, either. Research has found that shame can be one of the most powerful drivers of individual behavioral change.[17, 18]

Shame strikes directly at our innate need for social acceptance, and carries the threat of being outcast from the group. In order to feel psychologically secure, an individual targeted with a shame campaign will have to make amends in some way to restore their place in the group, and this process often involves significant self-reflection.

Shame-based approaches focus on direct confrontation with the individuals and organizations involved in your challenge. These campaigns are attempts to hit your targets where they hurt: their customer base, their voters, their employees, their neighbors, etc. Generally, these approaches use unpleasant truths as the basis to start attacking an organization's reputation while counting on a public relations snowball to build as more media outlets pick up the issue and add pressure.

This approach also carries risk. What causes shame to one person may have no effect on another, and some organizations have significant resources to fight back against public opinion. A campaign based on ridicule, exposure of lies, blunt opinions, and other tools of shame can also create negative perceptions of your organization as well.

Case Study: Greenpeace

Greenpeace began as an antinuclear movement in the 1970s, and has since expanded its "direct action" protest efforts against a number of environmental threats. The organization designs its tactics to generate maximum attention on specific company practices and individuals who are not living up to environmental standards in order to shame them into action.

In 2011, Greenpeace began a "Detox my Fashion" campaign to highlight the pollution impact of chemicals used by the fabric and fashion industry on the global water supply. The campaign included video and images of toxic effluent from manufacturing plants, along with petitions and protest actions of individuals competing against each other wearing apparel from major athletic brands such as Nike, Adidas, and others with "Detox" branding on top of the manufacturers' marks. The campaign secured pledges from 80 brands to eliminate chemical use by 2020, and later follow-ups by Greenpeace, designed to prevent greenwashing by keeping the pressure on those brands, found significant progress.

Research conducted on the campaign found that much of the attention generated drove consumers to reconsider their purchase choices, which in turn drove the brands to act.[19]

Case Study: #MeToo

The #MeToo awareness campaign against sexual harassment and assault began in 2006, but gained significant public awareness during the initial exposure of film producer Harvey Weinstein's sexual assault allegations in 2017. Numerous claims and prosecutions of other executives and celebrities followed, with reports of sexual harassment surging the following year[20] and hundreds of individuals losing their jobs[21] in a new climate of scrutiny and support for those wronged.

Control-Based Approaches

Co-Creation

When lack of control is the cause of your audience's fear, a concept called **co-creation** can be your best change approach.

Co-creation is the simple act of working on change together with the affected parties. Let's say, for example, you were lobbying for more electric cars. How are gas station owners going to make a living in a world where no one needs to fill up? Perhaps you could work with them to install charging stations and more waiting lounges to increase revenue while travelers wait to top off their batteries.

This approach to joint problem solving helps affected individuals recover autonomy and reorient their identity by involving them in the decision-making around a change. This approach lets affected individuals build a psychological safe zone, and potentially become even bigger advocates for your efforts since they have developed an ownership stake in the change, and a portion of their identities is now tied to the success of the endeavor.[22]

Another benefit of co-creation is that it sidesteps issues of media and advertising resources in favor of direct interaction. While this "door-to-door" effort can take time, it also builds relationships and trust, which can help pave the way for significant future breakthroughs.

Resistance Factor 3: Inertia

One of my favorite case studies comes from a friend who has spent his career in the consumer packaged-goods industry. After a change to one of the products he managed, his company received so many complaints that the change started to receive national media coverage. When I reached out to ask him what happened, his response was enlightening. His company had decades of statistics showing that whenever a change was made to a product, be it new packaging, a new formula, etc., the company would receive a wave of complaints, followed by an upswing in sales after the market finally accepted the change.

One small product change disrupted the routines of millions of purchasers, creating a large negative reaction.

We all enjoy the comfort of routine. A warm cup of coffee, a morning walk, a good book at the end of a long day. Our minds crave this consistency, because it reduces the metabolic load of unpacking a novel experience. We try out all kinds of different approaches when we're first learning, but eventually settle into a predictable pattern that lets us put our brains on autopilot. Those habits deepen over time like a mental rut in the road, and when we encounter a potential change, we resist it because change causes us some level of discomfort, even if it is small or improves our lives.[23]

On a macro level, you are likely trying to change a system that was created by others before you. That system would not be working as it was unless it was operating to the benefit of the majority of participants (even if the benefit is that it's familiar), and is created by some mix of:

- Past experiences
- Cultural norms (social standing, religious teachings, historical circumstances, etc.)
- Pressure to conform, which could be cultural, legal, etc.
- Economic interests
- Political considerations

The immense weight of these factors will bend society toward stasis, because the time and effort it takes to change them will come at a direct cost to some of its stakeholders and constituents (social inertia is often motivated by a desire to maintain control and protect vested interests). These costs could range from higher taxes to shifting resources away from special interests, or more onerous regulations that raise the cost of compliance. And existing market participants will be heavily invested in resisting them.

Reversing Inertia

Inertia issues stem from two sources: individual habits and social inertia. Let's examine solutions for both.

Breaking Individual Habits

Remember the dopamine-driven arousal theory? A related concept called the **habit loop** looks at the mental stimuli and responses involved in our everyday decisions, and shows how to break out of the inertia rut. The habit loop involves the following cycle:

1. **Cue:** anything that triggers the habitual behavior
2. **Craving:** the learned motivational pressure that builds and also triggers dopamine
3. **Response:** your habitual action
4. **Reward:** the reinforcement you receive after your action[24]

This cycle becomes more psychologically challenging to break the longer it lasts, but it can be reversed. Breaking habitual inertia requires providing your audience with new goals, along with related routines and reinforcement mechanisms, to help them transition away from their existing cues.

What might this process look like?

Let's say you're advocating for cutting down on sugars and sweets to improve physical health. What if your office switched from doughnuts to fruit for morning meetings? What if you organized an after-hours workout session instead of a happy hour? These kinds of small actions can begin to turn the tide on habits.

Reversing Social Inertia

Addressing social inertia requires a more complex approach, but still involves a focus on behavioral rewards. Researchers have developed the concept of a social identity model of collective action (SIMCA) to identify the three main factors that drive individuals to push for collective action against injustice:

- **Identity:** identification with a group (that may have become politicized)
- **Injustice:** recognition that a perceived injustice has been done to the group
- **Efficacy:** belief that the group has the means to achieve change[25]

Combatting social inertia follows a similar process to the one outlined in Chapters 2–6: identify your audience, make them aware of their pain points and your solution, and motivate them to act. Isn't that convenient?

In particular, the retention strategies in Chapter 6 focus on building goals and tracking progress against them, which can become an important part of building efficacy.

Power Building

As much as we try to play nice, there may come a time when you'll have to play hardball to break through inertia and advance your cause. If you're facing entrenched opposition from interests with significant economic, social, or political power, you'll need to know how to pin them to the mat to get your way.

We will cover power building more extensively in Chapter 8.

WHAT RESISTANCE WILL YOU FACE?

As you promote your cause, it can be helpful to understand the different categories of resistance that typically manifest:

- Denial (of the problem)
- Opposition (to the solution)
- Lack of action

Denial of the Problem

To pervert Alcoholics Anonymous' famous saying, if you never admit to a problem, you'll never need to change.

Denial is a knee-jerk self-defense mechanism for many of us when we don't want to spend the time to truly address an issue. We'll downplay the problem, resort to tactics like gaslighting, or flat-out lie to try and avoid a painful admission or change.

While individual denial is certainly challenging, it can become much more threatening at scale.

For bigger issues, denial becomes a tactic to delay progress until the pressure for change disappears. A number of industries and executives have been caught using denial in the press, the courts, and Congress to try and block investigations, prevent legislation, or avoid regulation. Perhaps most famously, oil industry executives knew from their own internal research that their companies' actions had been causing climate change for decades, but repeatedly testified to the contrary in front of the public.[26]

Organizations often use disingenuous arguments when adopting denial tactics. The organizations and spokespeople involved are almost always well aware of the effect they're having on the issue you've identified. Their only goal is to prevent change. And they will lobby, attack, greenwash, and acquire as needed to preserve their economic edge.

All of this behavior is easy to identify and understand. The question is, how to counter it?

Countering Denial

These change management tactics can help counter denial:

- Education
- Shame and ridicule
- Power building

Opposition to the Solution

Once you're able to build enough of a consensus that a problem exists, stakeholders will begin calling for a solution. At this point, you'll start to see different oppositional tactics rise to the fore. These tactics can include both active and passive opposition.

Active Opposition

Protests, lobbying, cancel attempts, media blitzes, character attacks, attempts to discredit your research, and any number of other direct approaches comprise active opposition. You'll likely know you're a target as soon as someone tries it, but the source may surprise you. It might come from your competitors and other market stakeholders, or you may find yourself defending against an advocacy group you never knew existed.

Passive Opposition

Passive opposition can be slightly more insidious. It comes in the form of lip service, where the politically expedient thing to do is demonstrate concern but take no action, or greenwashing from a company that has just been shamed for a poor environmental track record. It may also come in the form of analysis paralysis, where stakeholders continually request more studies or additional research, knowing that additional data-gathering will only take more time and not make an answer any clearer. Passive opposition may even be well-intentioned at times, but it comes with an array of tactics and actions designed to slow down your progress and muddy the future waters.

Countering Opposition

Countering opposition requires strength. No matter how "right" your cause might be, no matter what the facts or research show, your opposition has made a choice to side against your rational, logical arguments. The tactics below seek to work around that opposition:

- Co-creation
- Power building
- Enthusiasm

Lack of Action

Have you heard of the pocket veto? The stars align for legislation to move forward, it reaches the president's desk and then . . . the president simply doesn't sign the bill? This kind of lack of action happens all the time. If you're lucky enough to move a solution forward, you'll likely find that not every stakeholder feels motivated to support your change.

These individuals haven't shown active opposition, but they haven't exactly been setting any hair on fire to execute the tasks required to make change. You've probably seen this behavior among employees, family members, and corporations who'd rather see an issue disappear than deal with it. So, they resist by conducting business as usual while trying to outlast the issue.

These change management tactics can help counter lack of action:

- Enthusiasm
- Habit-breaking

A BRIEF GUIDE TO CONQUERING RESISTANCE

The tactic grid below can serve as a guideline for when to deploy specific tactics to overcome change resistance.

	TYPE OF RESISTANCE		
Resistance Manifestation	**Ignorance**	**Fear**	**Inertia**
Denial	Education	Shame Power building	Power building Shame
Opposition	Education	Enthusiasm Co-creation	Enthusiasm SIMCA
Lack of Action	Awareness	Enthusiasm	Habit-breaking SIMCA

FINAL THOUGHTS: ON POWER AND CHANGE

Remember our learning from the beginning of this chapter: individual beliefs are much more malleable than we might assume. Which means that the core of resistance to change doesn't really come from individuals. It comes from other organizations.

Organized resistance to change comes in many forms, for many reasons. As you continue to expand your change efforts, that resistance will become more and more rooted in economics. And that economic resistance will drive more and more of the political decision-making surrounding your issue. Which means that your next stop in overcoming resistance is to figure out how you can build the power you need.

Maybe you think you're biting off more than you can chew at this point, and you might be right. But no examination of why good is hard would be complete if we didn't dabble in a little macroeconomics.

So let's move on to our final chapter, and learn how to flex our change muscles just a bit more.

8

Achieving the Power to Change

THE FINAL FRONTIER

A few years ago, I worked with a solar power installation company that was trying to get local regulatory approval for community solar cooperatives in its state. These cooperatives would allow anyone in a certain location to join, install solar panels, and benefit from localized access to clean energy, even if they didn't have the perfect roofline over their head.

At least, that was the vision. The reality was that a patchwork of state and local regulations, plus resistance from the utility companies, made solar co-ops quite difficult to enact.

My client, the business's founder, made significant policy progress in his home and adjoining counties. But he realized that if he wanted to push that change at a bigger scale, he'd need a bigger lever. So he ran for Congress. And he lost, badly. So badly, in fact, that he sold his business rather than continue pushing a vision he knew he couldn't achieve.

What did I learn from his experience? That enacting change at scale requires power.

When I'm working with someone who's trying to promote a change for good, they're generally humble, hardworking, and focused on making things better for those around them. They don't have any dreams of running for office, or becoming billionaires, or bending an industry to their will.

But their competitors do.

So in this last chapter, we're going to take off the gloves. If you're angry at continued injustice in our society, at the ongoing problems we fail to solve year after year and decade after decade, it's time to turn that anger into action. We're going to stand up for ourselves and shift the economic power balance in our favor.

We'll start with an overview of what exactly "power" means: how it's generated and who holds it. Then we'll review ways to grow your power in order to enact change—regardless of how the opposition feels.

So roll up your sleeves and get ready for a fight, because it's one thing to lobby the power company, but it's quite another to be its controlling shareholder.

WHAT IS POWER?

Humans have devoted much of our history to understanding and acquiring power. While subjects like Machiavelli and Genghis Khan are a bit outside this book's scope, for the purposes of enacting change we can classify the sources of societal power into four areas:

- **Compulsory:** The ability to directly force your will onto another through means like military or law enforcement action. Also known as "hard power."
- **Institutional:** Control of entities that govern the actions of a collective, such as branches of government, stock markets, educational systems, court systems, etc.
- **Structural:** Influence over social nodes and leaders that compel and perform work, such as investors, business owners, or class and caste systems.

- **Productive:** The ability to create or produce something useful in generating structural power.[1]

These power sources interact in a complex dynamic. For example, a government (institutional power) passes a regulation about how motor vehicles must be built and operated. Drivers who break that law will face legal action (compulsory power), while manufacturers (productive power) may lobby to change the regulation to benefit their profit margins in order to satisfy investors (structural power).

As you can see from the example above, another way of defining "power" is control of the market and the regulatory factors that shape it. Generally, these factors are biased toward incumbents who have the resources to generate awareness, capture market share, and lobby for changes that support their business models (remember, we warned you about the stacked deck back in Chapter 1). But this doesn't mean automatic defeat. It just means that you'll need to understand which mountains must be moved in order to influence the existing power structure, or take their power for yourself.

WHO HOLDS YOUR MARKET'S POWER?

When it comes to social change, research has identified specific types of power interactions that can be useful in understanding where to push for your solution:

- **Power over versus power to:** Can you compel someone else to enact a change (power over), or are you the one who can deliver it directly (power to)?
- **Centered versus diffused:** Does power reside in a single location (say with the president) or is it generated collectively (by the voters)?

- **Consensual versus conflictual:** How hard will you have to push to generate change? Do you need to do a little education to build an agreeable consensus, or will you need to raise an army to fight for your cause?
- **Constraining versus enabling:** Will you need to rein in a societal actor like a corporation, or provide that actor with additional control?
- **Quantity versus quality:** What type of power, and how much, is needed to accomplish your specific change? For example, a push for increased environmental improvement could involve legislation, financing for a new technology, or simply the purchase of land. Each one of these actions would require a different source of power.
- **Empowerment versus disempowerment:** Do the people involved in enacting change have the ability and confidence to deliver what is needed, or do they have reason for doubt?
- **Power in relation to knowledge:** Do those who seek change have an understanding of the social levers they need to pull in order to do so?[2]

As you can imagine, the market interactions between the sources of power described above can become quite complex. The good news is that you can use a tool called a "**power map**" to guide you.

Power Mapping

A power map is a visual representation of the key individuals and organizations that influence your market, their relationships, and their level of influence over each other. You can use this tool to identify your cause's target audience, potential allies, and opponents.

You build a power map by brainstorming every player involved in the value chain of your market, vetting that draft list through your market research, and then sketching out a visualization of those groups.

Example High-Level Power Map

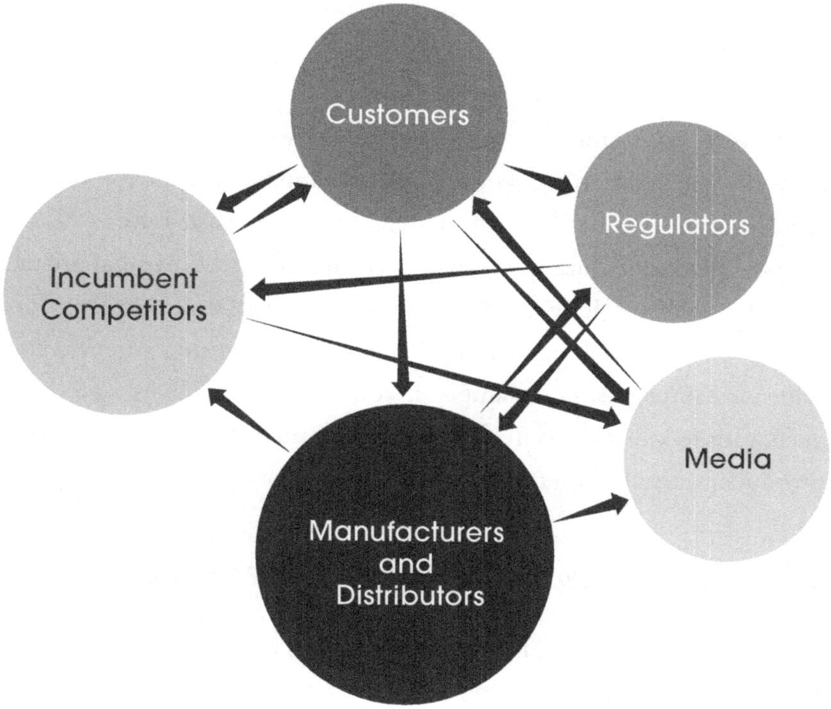

Any segment within the areas mentioned above that influences the information, revenue, or choices within a market should appear as a node on your power map. Groups that might appear on your power map could include:

- **Customers,** who hold the power of the purse and ultimately form the market
- **Regulators,** who shape the market to allow or incentivize certain solutions
- **Incumbent competitors,** who hold the power of awareness in the market along with some control over customers (through contractual relationships)
- **Media** (reviewers, trade press, influencers, etc.), which controls information and perception within a market

- **Manufacturers and distributors**, who control access to a product, either at its source or the manner in which it reaches the market

As you create your power map, note the power interactions between the nodes you've identified. For example, does an incumbent also control an association that works with manufacturers and distributors? That's a critical piece of information that might influence who you approach with your solution. It's a good idea to collect names and contact information for individuals at these nodes as well, for future awareness and influence campaigns. For example, if you have a green energy product, you'll want to know who's in charge of your local utility commission and introduce yourself to them.

Case Study: Approaching Regulated Markets

I recently helped a client that was developing a new training software for first responders. During the course of our market research and power mapping, we discovered a few valuable pieces of information:

- Local municipalities generally set their own first responder budgets, but states, cities, and counties have different size thresholds for purchases that require a public request for proposal (RFP).
- Existing incumbents provided expensive systems with high per-user license costs. They generally secured business by responding to RFPs.
- Federal first responder training centers often have "train the trainer" programs for state officials, who then return to their state and train local officials.

What did we do with this information?

- We set our entry price for a five-user license below the most common minimum RFP threshold, so that any department would have a financial incentive to try and (hopefully) buy the software without a lengthy proposal process that would expose us to competition.
- We used our low entry price to earn goodwill and demonstrate our cost-driven value proposition (virtual training costs a fraction of live training).
- We focused our limited marketing and business development resources on building relationships with federal training centers in order to collect feedback and gain endorsements from these groups, which would trickle down to state and local jurisdictions and generate demand for our product.

The result is a thriving business that has exited the "startup" phase of its existence and is well on its way to building staying power in the industry. All thanks to knowing how to use a power map.

BUILDING POWER TO CHANGE

If you don't seek economic power on your change journey, you're doomed to repeat the same Sisyphean battle as my conversational counterpart from Chapter 1, where the best you can hope for is scrounging up enough influence to add a few sentences to a draft regulation.

If you've gotten this far, I would encourage you to consider turning your solution into a for-profit business that takes advantage of the capitalistic levers our society has seen fit to enshrine in law. Doing so will give you the ability to influence your market's power interactions and drive true change.

Let's explore a few ways to accumulate this power.

Capital

True market power generally requires a significant amount of capital. Capital is the grease that moves our economy and gives us the ability to compel work from others. You can access or create capital in a number of ways, such as seeking investors, earning returns on investments, applying for loans and grants, or generating revenue from your solution.

When seeking to grow capital, understand that you will need healthy financials or the prospect of solid returns in order to build this element of your power. If you've done your homework properly from this book, you'll be in great shape. You'll have a well-defined potential market opportunity along with a unique value proposition that will position you to capture share. But you'll also need to put significant work into your financials to build a strong operational path that leads to profit growth and returns for your investors.

There is good news in this space: research shows that companies focusing on environmental, social, and governance (ESG) metrics tend to outperform the market.[3] And it is very likely that your solution will attract powerful financial tailwinds by focusing on reducing "societal overhead"—excessive market costs due to existing inefficiencies.

The most notable of these examples in the US may be health care, where a fierce debate rages over how to bring down costs for a system that comprises 17.6 percent of US GDP.[4] To no surprise, venture capital senses an opportunity to increase efficiency in the category while generating solid returns, and has flooded into the health sector.[5]

Adding capital to your organization's balance sheet is one thing. If you're seeking more power, however, look for opportunities to gather larger amounts of capital and direct it to your good cause. Those activities could look like the following:

- **Establishment of ESG funds and investment vehicles:** This trend is already well under way, with the first socially focused fund established in 1971 and the market currently featuring offerings from major mutual fund providers like Vanguard and BlackRock.

- **Creation of change-focused banks and sources of capital:** States and communities regularly establish socially focused banks, and this trend appears to be accelerating with the creation of the first national "green" bank by the Coalition for Green Capital in 2024.
- **Collective local investment:** These initiatives could take the shape of incubators, grants, and public-private partnerships to address local economic issues and improve collective living conditions.
- **Changes to taxation and financing terms:** Tax codes can be updated to incentivize market behavior, and preferential financing can be offered to businesses that meet certain social criteria.

You have the opportunity to direct and shape these vehicles by presenting investment opportunities and generating revenue through your change efforts. And you could, of course, create your own source of change capital. You might not ever reach the scale of BlackRock, but you don't have to. Americans already give $474 billion annually to charities[6]—if you're able to collect a fraction of that generosity, you'll have a healthy bankroll for your change efforts.

Market Participants

Those who control market factors like production, distribution, preference, and choice wield significant power. As an example, let's examine food prices. USDA research has found that food suppliers have seen 94 percent market consolation in food retailers since 1990.[7] As a result, grocery prices have risen by 20 percent since 2018, while simultaneously pushing down prices paid to the farmers actually producing the food.[8]

As a particular example, just four companies control 85 percent of beef packing in the US.[9]

So, when you go to the grocery store and wince at the prices, understand that those prices aren't coming from the farmers. They're coming from every other step of the distribution chain, which is growing more and more consolidated.

How do we stop this? By providing alternatives. Of course, we're not all in agriculture, but let's use this industry as an example of how power acquisition among market participants might work.

Farmers produce a crop with a variable yield and price that must be quickly sold and processed at regular times each year. As such, they are at the mercy of not only the weather and seed prices, but the price that processors and distributors are willing to pay. When markets consolidate around them, they have very little recourse to change their situation. What options do we have to shift the power dynamic in this industry?

- **Consolidation:** If enough suppliers band together, they can achieve the power to negotiate better prices. This is often done by cooperatives of growers, like Blue Diamond or Ocean Spray.
- **Direct distribution:** Suppliers and manufacturers can sell directly to end customers. They might have to take on some processing, marketing, and shipping costs, but those expenses may be worth it to capture market share.
- **Vertical integration:** Going a step further, farms could expand into the processing, packaging, and distribution of their products in order to capture and deliver more market value. You see this approach in large players like Tyson Foods.
- **End customer marketing (or ingredient branding):** Upstream producers can often state their case directly to end customers via marketing in order to build market preference for their product. The "Got Milk" campaign is a famous example of end customer marketing.

- **Microproduction:** The opposite of mass production, microfarms have been cropping up closer to their end markets in cities such as Detroit, with niche practices like vertical farming. The goal of these initiatives is to develop a product closer to its consumer to reduce the number of middlemen.

These are just a few ways to gain power by influencing and shaping market participants. And they aren't just limited to agriculture.

Case Study: REI Co-op

One way to unite market participants is through a co-op, which unites producers and consumers in a shared relationship that can move beyond profit. Outdoor equipment retailer REI, for example, offers co-op membership to all of its customers, going so far as allowing members to vote for the co-op's board of directors (as well as nominate themselves for those positions). Co-op members receive discounts and opportunities to participate in unique experiences and deals. This collective ownership model has resonated with consumers to the tune of $3.7 billion in annual revenue, alongside support for a number of venture funds and other activities to support conservation and outdoor activities.

Notes on Disruption and Zero-Sum Theory

You've likely heard a lot about "disrupting" particular industries in the past few years, as companies ranging from Uber to sports drink brands try to attract excitement and investment. And by now you know that markets will resist disruption with every fiber of their existence.

These incumbents are operating from a zero-sum mindset, in which one winner must ultimately take all. This mindset is highly prevalent in business because, as my client trying to sell recycled cups realized, someone will win the contract, and someone else won't.

But what if we could be more cooperative?

I bring this up because those of us supporting causes are going to have to present multiple value propositions to different audiences with different levels of market power, including our customers, our staff, local politicians, suppliers, and others.

The ideal value proposition from another market participant's viewpoint is a win-win for both parties, as opposed to a zero-sum approach. If you have a more efficient way of delivering a service to a customer, perhaps you can partner with industry groups and associations to expand your customer base, and with other members of your value chain to expand your capacity.

The point is that if you focus on delivering as much value to as broad a constituency as possible, at a fair price, you'll be better positioned for long-term success than if you approach things from an all-or-nothing viewpoint. Remember, you're trying to cultivate and share power and influence within existing networks, not burn them all to the ground.

Resource Owners

The modern economy places heavy demands on natural and human resources. Physical products require resources like oil and lumber, software requires vast power consumption to run its data centers, and service industries require significant contributions from their workforce. If you can control these resource inputs, you will hold power.

As an example, let's look at the water and electricity required in today's data-center-heavy climate. Each year, data centers use 2 percent of the nation's entire electrical output, and 174 billion gallons of water. Which means they sit in a difficult position between the communities in which they're built and the organizations that need to use them to generate an economic return. This tension is leading to an increase in protests against data center construction.[10] So how can we assert control in this dynamic?

- **Regulation:** Political power is often one of the first ways organizations seek to control resource owners. In our data center example, we could impose requirements on data centers' usage of water and electricity, such as Virginia's efforts to require renewable energy use for all data centers. We could also impose requirements on land sales to prevent certain densities.
- **Innovation:** Creating new resources or inputs for a process can improve efficiencies and lessen the resource pressure required. For example, focusing on clean energy generation or cutting-edge technologies like supercooled micro data centers or DNA data storage could provide more resilient paths forward.
- **Unions:** Workers are a resource, and the power of collective bargaining has given American workers strong benefits in a number of industries where specialized, skilled workers are not easily replaced.
- **Knowledge:** Intellectual property, patents, blueprints, software, and other knowledge tools that enable efficiency can be preferentially provided to deliver social change through licensing or other usage rights.
- **Certifications:** Certification authorities can ensure that resource owners produce and harvest their outputs in a way that meets an acceptable standard.

When thinking about resource power, understanding power interactions will be critical to identifying exactly how you can go about consolidating power over either the resource owners or the resources themselves.

WHAT ABOUT POLITICAL POWER?

You'll note that the above discussions don't focus on political power. And I'm assuming you're not interested in becoming a dictator, so we haven't touched much on compulsory power either.

If you have the ability to advance your cause through political influence, by all means, do it. The thesis of this book, based on my own experience, is that economic power drives political power.

Consider climate change denial. Despite scientific consensus that our planet is warming, 28 percent of Congress has cast doubt on climate change. These lawmakers do not truly doubt the science. They do it because their funding comes from a small number of corporations and ultra-wealthy owners in industries that benefit from lobbying against climate change, such as Exxon Mobil and Koch Industries.[11, 12, 13]

Would you be able to outspend these donors? If you can, fighting a two-front war on the commercial and political fronts can only help. But if you can't, I recommend focusing on commercial solutions that can be used to build economic power. At some point in the future, your economic power will become political power.

FINAL THOUGHTS

You might be familiar with the "Great Man theory," which states that true societal change requires an individual with extraordinary vision to lead humanity in a new direction. Modern scholars tend to reject this theory in favor of a combination of external and internal factors that affect people at all levels of society and drive some to act. Some of those actors do become "great," but they would not have been able to harness collective action if the conditions had not been ripe in the first place. In reality, as the saying goes, change happens gradually, on many fronts, and then all at once.

So, while there is no easy path to gaining market power, every step you take in its direction will help a tiny pebble of change turn into a landslide.

Our lessons in this chapter are less tactical than others, because no one path to power exists. It's best to set a goal and work toward it as your solution matures, rather than build a specific plan that may change as market influence shifts. Maybe you start by convening an informal industry group, or maybe you talk to the local mayor's office.

Whatever the steps required, just make sure you find the time and summon the will to take them.

As fans of the free market like to say, customers have a choice, and that choice will drive the market. When it comes to market power, you must become the better alternative to the status quo if you want to drive change. Because if you don't, someone else will.

Closing

My fear as I've worked on this book is that I might be presenting the path to doing good as too hard. You'll face a lot of headwinds, but they are by no means too strong for you to handle. In spite of all the challenges we've just covered, my hope is that you'll feel optimistic about your path forward.

As I write this, the American economy has been on an incredible run of business starts, adding somewhere between 300,000 and 500,000 new businesses every quarter since the COVID-19 pandemic.[14] While many of these business starts may be from "necessity entrepreneurship" to support individuals who have been laid off, it is striking that business start rates are running close to double that of the past 20 years.

This gives me an incredible amount of hope. But in case you're not feeling the same, I want to share one last insight with you.

No matter what your cause may be, you will feel frustrated about solving your issue at some point, thanks to intractable social problems, human nature, political opposition, economics, or any number of mountains standing in the way.

Change management professionals developed the concept of the Emotional Cycle of Change in the late 1970s[15] to describe this phenomenon, and it looks something like this:

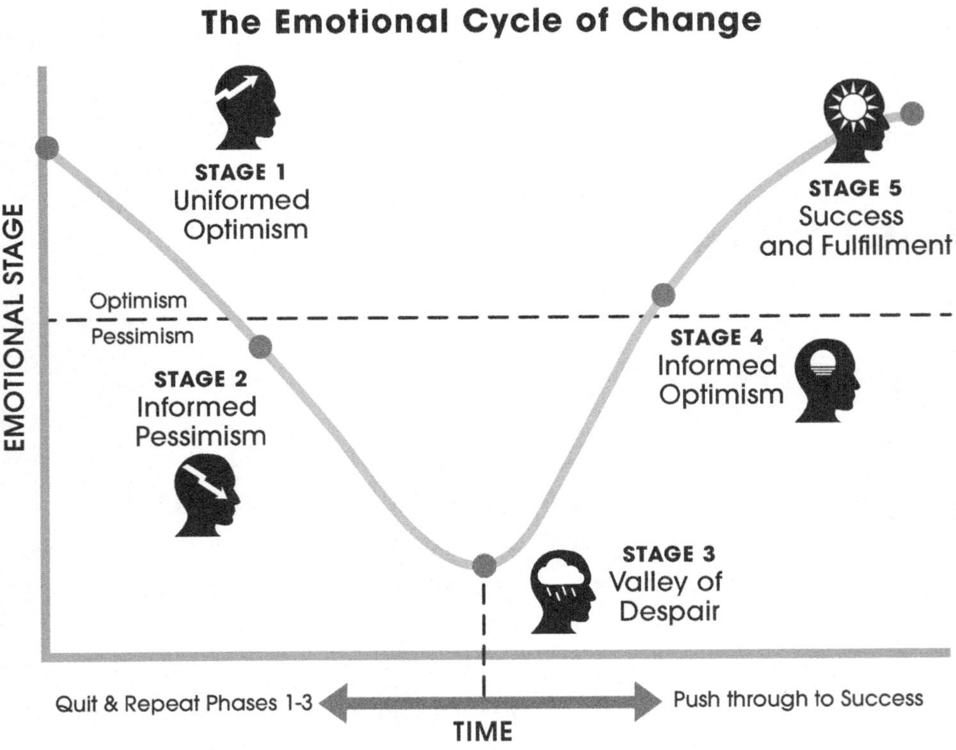

Once the initial excitement of starting something new wears off and we realize the extent of work required to actually solve our challenge, we reach a stage called "informed pessimism." If you internalized the lesson in Chapter 6 about setting SMART goals, you and your audience will have started chipping away at realistic achievements and moving your solution forward. But inevitably, you'll encounter issues.

Low response rates, a lack of resources, grant funding that doesn't come through, unhappy customers, and any number of other challenges will occur. And as they pile up, it can be easy to throw up your hands and quit. This is the "valley of despair," and I've encountered it on nearly every large project I've taken on (including the writing of this book).

The valley of despair is also where grit can save us. Despite the odds, we're going to push through and succeed. No matter what stands in our way, we're going to find another gear and climb our mountain.

Every successful change starts with a person and an idea. If you're tired of the way things are and want to see the world improve, there's no better time to do so than right now.

Remember the person in charge of packaging I met back in Chapter 1 who was too afraid to start his own business? A different type of person would stand up and pound the table for real change. And if his superiors told them to pipe down because they couldn't lose the fraction of a penny in profit that the change would require, a different type of person might quit to start their own packaging company.

I want you to be that different type of person. It is time for us to stop talking and take the hard steps required to solve problems and make real change.

We only get one spin around this earth, so we don't have any more time to waste. It's time to make an impact that counts, before it's too late.

I know you will, and I thank you for allowing me to be a part of your journey.

Notes

Chapter 1

1. "8 Theories of Motivation and Human Desire," Chopra, September 5, 2018, https://web.archive.org/web/20240703183302/https://chopra.cfootom/blogs/personal-growth/8-theories-of-motivation-and-human-desire.

2. Neel Burton, "An Analysis of Altruism," *Psychology Today*, June 23, 2024, https://www.psychologytoday.com/us/blog/hide-and-seek/201203/does-true-altruism-exist.

3. Ireneusz Rutkowski, "Success and failure rates of new food and non-food products introduced on the market," *Journal of Marketing and Consumer Behaviour in Emerging Markets* 1 (April 2022): 52–61, https://www.researchgate.net/publication/359923834_Success_and_failure_rates_of_new_food_and_non-food_products_introduced_on_the_market.

4. "What Percentage of Small Businesses Fail? 2025 Data Reveals the Answer," Commerce Institute, November 15, 2025, https://www.commerceinstitute.com/business-failure-rate.

5. "Why today's pricing is sabotaging sustainability," Kearney, September 11, 2020, https://www.kearney.com/industry/consumer-retail/article/-/insights/why-todays-pricing-is-sabotaging-sustainability.

6. Andrea K. Moser, "Thinking Green, Buying Green? Drivers of Pro-environmental Purchasing Behavior." *Journal of Consumer Marketing* 32, no. 3 (May 5, 2015): 167–75, https://doi.org/10.1108/jcm-10-2014-1179.

7. Ashley Lobo, "Case Study of Toyota Prius – The world's most popular Hybrid Electric Vehicle," March 18, 2020, https://www.linkedin.com/pulse/case-study-toyota-prius-worlds-most-popular-hybrid-electric-lobo.

8. Alex Taylor III, "Toyota: The Birth of the Prius," *Fortune*, February 21, 2006, https://www.scribd.com/document/136692236/Toyota

9. Eylem Bulut et al., "Influence of Sustainability on the Purchase Decision of Products," *European Journal of Applied Business and Management* 8, no. 3 (September 30, 2022), https://nidisag.isag.pt/index.php/IJAM/article/view/634.

10. Paul Clolery, "Study: Nonprofits Spending Billions on Ads, Promotion," The NonProfit Times, November 3, 2021, https://thenonprofittimes.com/npt_articles/study-nonprofits-spending-billions-on-ads-promotion.

11. J.G. Navarro, "Ad Spending in Selected Markets Worldwide 2025," Statista, February 3, 2026, https://www.statista.com/forecasts/1380173/ad-spending-markets-worldwide.

12. Rachelle C. Sampson and Yuan Shi, "Are US Firms Becoming More Short-Term Oriented? Evidence of Shifting Firm Time Horizons from Implied Discount Rates, 1980-2013," *Strategic Management Journal*, October 1, 2019, https://papers.ssrn.com/sol3/papers.cfm?abstract_id=2837524.

13. Cory Doctorow, "The 'Enshittification' of TikTok," *Wired*, January 23, 2023, https://www.wired.com/story/tiktok-platforms-cory-doctorow.

14. Dave Pollard, "Why Unregulated Capitalism Always Leads to Enshittification," How to Save the World, May 11, 2024, https://howtosavetheworld.ca/2024/05/11/why-unregulated-capitalism-always-leads-to-enshittification.

Chapter 2

1. Tiago Bianchi, "Online Search Market Worldwide," Statista, December 17, 2025, https://www.statista.com/topics/1710/search-engine-usage/#topicOverview.

2. "Men vs. Women: Car Buying Infographic," CJ Pony Parts, Accessed January 2, 2025, https://www.cjponyparts.com/media/images/blog/men-vs-women-car-buying-infographic.jpg.

3. Kea Wilson, "SUV And Pickup Purchases Soar — but Who's Buying?" Streetsblog USA, May 31, 2023, https://usa.streetsblog.org/2021/04/21/suv-and-pickup-purchases-soar-but-whos-buying.

4. "As their sales continue to rise, SUVs' global CO2 emissions are nearing 1 billion tonnes," International Energy Agency, February 27, 2023, https://www.iea.org/commentaries/as-their-sales-continue-to-rise-suvs-global-co2-emissions-are-nearing-1-billion-tonnes.

5. "Men vs. Women: Car Buying Infographic."

6. Vivek Gupta and A. Harish, "Nike 'Considered': An Environmental Sustainability Initiative," *IBS Center for Management Research*, 2010, https://www.ibscdc.org/Case_Studies/Business%20Ethics/Business%20Ethics/BECG111.htm.

7. Rebecca Henderson et al., "Nike Considered: Getting Traction on Sustainability," MIT Management Sloan School, January 21, 2009, https://mitsloan.mit.edu/sites/default/files/2024-04/Nike%20Considered.pdf.

Chapter 3

1. "Segway," Wikimedia Foundation, last modified January 28, 2026, https://en.wikipedia.org/wiki/Segway.

2. "Segway Case: Poor Value Proposition," Drew (blog), July 10, 2022, https://blog.wearedrew.co/en/segway-case-poor-value-proposition.

3. "Segway Case Study: Avoiding the Fate of the Segway Electric Scooter," Blue Ocean Strategy, May 26, 2022, https://www.blueoceanstrategy.com/blog/segway-case-study-avoiding-fate-of-segway-electric-scooter.

4. Matt McFarland, "Segway was supposed to change the world. Two decades later, it just might," *CNN*, October 30, 2018, https://edition.cnn.com/2018/10/30/tech/segway-history/index.html.

5. Katie Surma, "The Deteriorating Environment Is a Public Concern, but Americans Misunderstand Their Contribution to the Problem," Inside Climate News, September 5, 2024, https://insideclimatenews.org/news/05092024/global-climate-concerns-survey.

6. Johnny Wood, "This is what stops people from recycling more, finds a global survey," World Economic Forum, November 18, 2021, https://www.weforum.org/stories/2021/11/barriers-to-recycling-sustainability-survey.

7. Xiayun Zhang and Feng Dong, "Why Do Consumers Make Green Purchase Decisions? Insights from a Systemic Review," *International Journal of Environmental Research and Public Health* 17, no. 18 (September 11, 2020): 6607, https://doi.org/10.3390/ijerph17186607.

8. Tom Swallow, "Top 10 B Corps Companies," *Sustainability Magazine*, January 4, 2024, https://sustainabilitymag.com/articles/top-10-b-corps.

9. Jeff Beer, "Exclusive: Patagonia Is in Business to Save Our Home Planet." *Fast Company*, December 13, 2018, https://www.fastcompany.com/90280950/exclusive-patagonia-is-in-business-to-save-our-home-planet.

10. Juliana Menasce Horowitz et al., "Support for the Black Lives Matter Movement Has Dropped Considerably from Its Peak in 2020," Pew Research Center, April 24, 2025, https://www.pewresearch.org/social-trends/2023/06/14/support-for-the-black-lives-matter-movement-has-dropped-considerably-from-its-peak-in-2020.

Chapter 4

1. Andrea I. Luppi et al., "A Synergistic Core for Human Brain Evolution and Cognition," *Nature Neuroscience* 25, no. 6 (May 26, 2022): 771–82, https://doi.org/10.1038/s41593-022-01070-0.

2. Bernt Bratsberg and Ole Rogeberg, "Flynn effect and its reversal are both environmentally caused," *Proceedings of the National Academy of Sciences* 115, no. 26 (June 11, 2018): 6674–78, https://www.pnas.org/doi/10.1073/pnas.1718793115.

3. Philipp Lorenz-Spreen, Bjarke Morch Monsted and Philipp Hovel, "Accelerating dynamics of collective attention," *Nature*, 15 April 2019, https://www.nature.com/articles/s41467-019-09311-w

4. Simon Maybin, "Busting the Attention Span Myth," *BBC News*, March 10, 2017, https://www.bbc.com/news/health-38896790.

5. Sjoerd Lops, "Consumer Attention and Its Importance for Paid Media," Artefact, September 20, 2024, https://www.artefact.com/blog/consumer-attention-and-its-importance-for-paid-media.

6. Tatevik Mkrtchyan, "Media Execs Can't Afford to Sleep on Attention." Digital Content Next, June 20, 2023, https://digitalcontentnext.org/blog/2023/06/20/media-execs-cant-afford-to-sleep-on-attention.

7. Mkrtchyan, "Media Execs Can't Afford to Sleep on Attention."

8. Vaughn Bell, "Don't Touch That Dial! A History of Media Technology Scares, from the Printing Press to Facebook," *Slate,* February 23, 2010, https://slate.com/technology/2010/02/a-history-of-media-technology-scares-from-the-printing-press-to-facebook.html.

9. Jesse Holcomb and Amy Mitchell, "The Revenue Picture for American Journalism and How It Is Changing," Pew Research Center, March 26, 2014, https://www.pewresearch.org/journalism/2014/03/26/the-revenue-picture-for-american-journalism-and-how-it-is-changing.

10. Chun-Yao Huang et al., "Concentration of Web users' online information behaviour," *Information Research* 12, no. 4 (October 2007), https://informationr.net/ir/12-4/paper324.html.

11. "Largest Media Companies Worldwide," Statista, November 27, 2025, https://www.statista.com/statistics/272469/largest-media-companies-worldwide.

12. "Search Engine Usage," Statista, December 17, 2025, https://www.statista.com/topics/1710/search-engine-usage.

13. Monique Solomons, "90 YouTube Statistics: revenue, marketing, and content," Linearity, March 20, 2024, https://www.linearity.io/blog/youtube-statistics/

14. Thuy D., "Cumulative number of daily Meta product users from 4th quarter 2018 to 4th quarter 2025," Statista, February 2, 2026, https://www.statista.com/statistics/1092227/facebook-product-dau.

15. "Comcast," Wikimedia Foundation, last modified February 8, 2026, https://en.wikipedia.org/wiki/Comcast.

16. Nic Newman, "Overview and key findings of the 2023 Digital News report," Reuters Institute, June 14, 2023, https://reutersinstitute.politics.ox.ac.uk/digital-news-report/2023/dnr-executive-summary.

17. Anton Ioffe, "YouTube Dominates TV Streaming in the US, per Nielsen's Latest Report," Borstch, February 20, 2024, https://borstch.com/blog/startup/youtube-dominates-tv-streaming-in-us-per-nielsens-latest-report.

18. Anne Steele, "A Few Blockbuster Podcasts Are Making All the Money," July 27, 2024, https://www.wsj.com/business/media/a-few-blockbuster-podcasts-are-making-all-the-money-d9cee36e.

19. Clolery, "Study: Nonprofits Spending Billions on Ads, Promotion."

20. Katie Jones, "How Total Spend by U.S. Advertisers Has Changed, Over 20 Years," Visual Capitalist, October 16, 2020, https://www.visualcapitalist.com/us-advertisers-spend-20-years.

21. Abigail Bosze, "U.S. Media Consumption (2018-2024)," Doofinder, March 18, 2025, https://www.doofinder.com/en/statistics/us-media-consumption.

22. David Brooks, "Despite Everything You Think You Know, America Is on the Right Track," *The Atlantic*, January 13, 2023, https://www.theatlantic.com/ideas/archive/2023/01/american-optimism-productivity-innovation-rise/672714.

23. Estela Saquete et al., "Why are some social-media contents more popular than others? Opinion and association rules mining applied to virality patterns discovery," *Expert Systems with Applications* 197 (July 1, 2022), https://www.sciencedirect.com/science/article/pii/S0957417422001609.

24. James H. Fowler and Nicholas A. Christakis, "Dynamic spread of happiness in a large social network: longitudinal analysis over 20 years in the Framingham Heart Study," *The BMJ Journal* 337 (December 5, 2008). https://www.bmj.com/content/337/bmj.a2338.short.

25. Adam D. I. Kramer et al., "Experimental Evidence of Massive-Scale Emotional Contagion Through Social Networks," *Proceedings of the National Academy of Sciences* 111, no. 24 (June 2, 2014): 8788–8790, https://www.pnas.org/doi/10.1073/pnas.1320040111.

26. Matt Binder, "The majority of traffic from Elon Musk's X may have been fake during the Super Bowl, report suggests," *Mashable*, February 16, 2024, https://mashable.com/article/x-twitter-elon-musk-bots-fake-traffic.

27. Ron Dicker, "Supercut of Sinclair TV Stations Reading Same Biden Slam Is a Repeat Offender," *HuffPost*, June 12, 2024, https://www.huffpost.com/entry/sinclair-tv-stations-joe-biden-wall-street-journal_n_6669a8dfe4b076909e1cc023.

28. William J. Brady, et al., "How social learning amplifies moral outrage expression in online social networks," *Science Advances* 7, no. 33 (August 13, 2021), https://www.science.org/doi/10.1126/sciadv.abe5641.

29. Adam P. Stern, "The Psychology of Internet Rage," *Harvard Health Publishing*, May 17, 2018, https://www.health.harvard.edu/blog/the-psychology-of-internet-rage-2018051713852.

30. T.J. Raphael, "The World Is Actually Safer Than Ever. And Here's the Data to Prove That," *The World*, October 23, 2014, https://theworld.org/stories/2014/10/23/world-actually-safer-ever-and-heres-data-prove.

31. John Gramlich, "What the Data Says About Crime in the U.S.," Pew Research Center, April 24, 2024, https://www.pewresearch.org/short-reads/2024/04/24/what-the-data-says-about-crime-in-the-us.

32. U.S. Energy Information Administration, "U.S. Electricity Generation from Renewables Surpassed Coal in April," Today in Energy, June 26, 2019, https://www.eia.gov/todayinenergy/detail.php?id=39992.

33. "National Household Travel Survey Daily Travel Quick Facts," Bureau of Transportation Statistics, May 31, 2017, https://www.bts.gov/statistical-products/surveys/national-household-travel-survey-daily-travel-quick-facts.

34. National Center for Statistics and Analysis, "Traffic Safety Facts: 2021 Data," National Highway Traffic Safety Administration, March 2022, https://crashstats.nhtsa.dot.gov/Api/Public/ViewPublication/813515.

35. Nasir Naqvi et al., "The Role of Emotion in Decision Making: A Cognitive Neuroscience Perspective," *Journal on the Psychological Science* 15, no. 5 (2006), https://journals.sagepub.com/doi/abs/10.1111/j.1467-8721.2006.00448.x.

36. Matt Abrahams, host, *Think Fast Talk Smart,* episode 24, "Feelings First: How Emotion Shapes Our Communication, Decisions, and Experiences," Stanford Graduate School of Business, November 20, 2020, https://www.gsb.stanford.edu/insights/feelings-first-how-emotion-shapes-communication-decisions-experiences.

37. Jennifer S. Lerner et al., "Emotion and Decision Making," *Annual Review of Psychology* 66 (2015): 799–823, accessed January 2, 2025, https://jenniferlerner.com/wp-content/uploads/2017/08/5.Emotion-and-Decision-Making.pdf.

38. Julian Kiverstein and Mark Miller, "The embodied brain: towards a radical embodied cognitive neuroscience," *Frontiers in Human Neuroscience* 9 (May 6, 2015), https://www.frontiersin.org/journals/human-neuroscience/articles/10.3389/fnhum.2015.00237/full.

39. Charley M. Wu et al., "Time pressure changes how people explore and respond to uncertainty," *Scientific Reports* 12 (March 8, 2022), https://www.nature.com/articles/s41598-022-07901-1

40. Brendan Nyhan and Jason Reifler, "When Corrections Fail: The Persistence of Political Misperceptions," *Political Behavior* 32 (March 30, 2010): 303–330, https://link.springer.com/article/10.1007/s11109-010-9112-2.

41. David Vrtana and Anna Krizanova, "The Power of Emotional Advertising Appeals: Examining Their Influence on Consumer Purchasing Behavior and Brand–Customer Relationship," *Sustainability* 15, no. 18 (September 6, 2023), https://www.mdpi.com/2071-1050/15/18/13337.

42. Edoardo Maria Polo et al., "Understanding the role of emotion in decision making process: using machine learning to analyze physiological responses to visual, auditory, and combined stimulation," *Frontiers in Human Neuroscience* 17 (January 8, 2024), https://www.frontiersin.org/journals/human-neuroscience/articles/10.3389/fnhum.2023.1286621/full.

43. Jennifer S. Lerner et al., "Emotion and Decision Making."

44. Diego Gomez-Carmona et al., "The effectiveness of environmental advertising: an analysis of advertising memory through neuroscience," *ICONO 14* 20, no. 2 (September 13, 2022), https://icono14.net/files/articles/1816-EN/index.html.

45. Nic Newman, "Overview and key findings of the 2022 Digital News Report," The Reuters Institute, June 15, 2022, https://reutersinstitute.politics.ox.ac.uk/digital-news-report/2022/dnr-executive-summary.

46. Jonah Berger and Katherine L. Milkman, "Social Transmission, Emotion, and the Virality of Online Content," *Marketing Science Institute Working Paper Series 2010*, January 1, 2010, https://thearf-org-unified-admin.s3.amazonaws.com/MSI/2020/06/MSI_Report_10-114.pdf.

47. Jonah Berger and Katherine L. Milkman, "What Makes Online Content Viral?," *Journal of Marketing Research* 49, no. 2 (April 1, 2012), https://journals.sagepub.com/doi/10.1509/jmr.10.0353.

48. Kevan Lee, "Want to Improve Your Social Media Sharing? Harness the Power of Positivity in Social Media," Buffer, October 16, 2014, https://buffer.com/resources/positivity-social-media.

49. Krzysztof Stepaniuk and Katarzyna Jarosz, "Persuasive linguistic tricks in social media marketing communication—The memetic approach," *PLOS ONE* 16, no. 7 (July 1, 2021), https://journals.plos.org/plosone/article?id=10.1371/journal.pone.0253983.

50. Hara Estroff Marano, "Why We Love Bad News," *Psychology Today*, May 27, 2003, https://www.psychologytoday.com/us/articles/200305/why-we-love-bad-news.

51. Jianming Wang et al., "The Impact of Positive Emotional Appeals on the Green Purchase Behavior," *Frontiers in Psychology* 13 (June 2, 2022), https://www.frontiersin.org/journals/psychology/articles/10.3389/fpsyg.2022.716027/full.

52. Jennifer S. Lerner et al., "Emotion and Decision Making."

53. Marcus Mayorga et al., "Comparing the Effect of Rational and Emotional Appeals on Donation Behavior," OSF, August 9, 2019, https://osf.io/bdnz2.

54. "Adults Spend Almost 10 Hours Per Day With The Media, But Note Only 150 Ads," *Media Dynamics Incorporated*, September 22, 2014, https://www.mediadynamicsinc.com/uploads/files/PR092214-Note-only-150-Ads-2mk.pdf.

55. Owen Gibson, "Shopper's eye view of ads that pass us by," *The Guardian,* November 19, 2005, https://www.theguardian.com/media/2005/nov/19/advertising.marketingandpr.

56. Susanne Schmidt and Martin Eisend, "Advertising Repetition: A Meta-Analysis on Effective Frequency in Advertising," *Journal of Advertising*

44, no. 4 (March 25, 2015): 415–428, https://www.tandfonline.com/doi/full/10.1080/00913367.2015.1018460.

57. Mya Frazier, "This Ad Will Give You a Headache, But It Sells," *Ad Age*, September 24, 2007, https://adage.com/article/news/ad-give-a-headache-sells/120636.

Chapter 5

1. Kelsey Snyder and Pashmeena Hilal, "The Changing Face of B2B Marketing," Think with Google, March 2015, https://www.thinkwithgoogle.com/_qs/documents/938/the-changing-face-b2b-marketing.pdf.

2. Breugelmans Els et al., "Calling Customers to Take Action: The Impact of Incentive and Customer Characteristics on Direct Mailing Effectiveness," *Journal of Interactive Marketing* 45, no. 1 (January 2018), https://www.researchgate.net/publication/329453846_Calling_Customers_to_Take_Action_The_Impact_of_Incentive_and_Customer_Characteristics_on_Direct_Mailing_Effectiveness.

3. Tser yeith Chen, "How different advertising formats and calls to action on videos affect advertising recognition and consequent behaviours," *The Service Industries Journal* 40, no. 1 (June 2018): 1–22, https://www.researchgate.net/publication/325560592_How_different_advertising_formats_and_calls_to_action_on_videos_affect_advertising_recognition_and_consequent_behaviours.

4. Myoung-Jin Chae, "Driving Consumer Engagement through Diverse Calls to Action in Corporate Social Responsibility Messages on Social Media," *Sustainability* 13, no. 7 (March 30, 2021), https://www.mdpi.com/2071-1050/13/7/3812.

5. "Car Allowance Rebate System," Wikimedia Foundation, last modified January 5, 2026, https://en.wikipedia.org/wiki/Car_Allowance_Rebate_System.

6. Matthew Wald, "In Congress, a Jump-Start for Clunkers," *The New York Times,* August 1, 2009, https://www.nytimes.com/2009/08/01/business/01clunkers.html.

7. Mei-Lan Lin et al., "The Psychological Motivations to Social Innovation and Transmitting Role of Social Worth," *Frontiers in Psychology* 13 (March 28, 2022), https://www.frontiersin.org/journals/psychology/articles/10.3389/fpsyg.2022.850783/full.

8. "Dawn Celebrates 40 Years of Helping Save Wildlife With #Dawnwildlife40," The Shorty Awards, accessed January 2, 2025, https://shortyawards.com/3rd-socialgood/dawn-celebrates-40-years-of-helping-save-wildlife-with-dawnwildlife40.

9 Stuart Mitchell, "Dawn Commemorates 40 Years of Helping Save Wildlife," Ethical Marketing News, July 28, 2018, https://ethicalmarketingnews.com/dawn-commemorates-40-years-of-helping-save-wildlife.

Chapter 6

1. Kiko Fronda, "The Hidden Perils of B2B Data Deprecation: A Marketer's Guide," DemandScience, March 14, 2024, https://demandscience.com/resources/blog/b2b-data-deprecation-marketers-guide.

2. Amy Gallo, "The Value of Keeping the Right Customers," *Harvard Business Review*, October 29, 2014, https://hbr.org/2014/10/the-value-of-keeping-the-right-customers.

3. Saksham Agarwal, "The Impact of Brand Relations and Consumer Characteristics on Brand Evangelism," *International Journal of Education and Science Research Review* 9, no. 4 (July-August 2022): 221–230, https://ijesrr.org/publication/88/5.%20july2022%20issn%20%20ijesrr.pdf.

4. "Consumer Trust in Online, Social and Mobile Advertising Grows," Nielsen, April 2012, https://www.nielsen.com/insights/2012/consumer-trust-in-online-social-and-mobile-advertising-grows.

5. Jacques Bughin et al., "A new way to measure word-of-mouth marketing," *McKinsey Quarterly*, April 1, 2010, https://www.mckinsey.com/capabilities/growth-marketing-and-sales/our-insights/a-new-way-to-measure-word-of-mouth-marketing.

6. "Purpose & Company Vision," The Coca-Cola Company, accessed January 2, 2025, https://www.coca-colacompany.com/about-us/purpose-and-vision.

7. Marta Zaraska, "Food Can Be Literally Addictive, New Evidence Suggests," *Scientific American,* September 11, 2023, https://www.scientificamerican.com/article/food-can-be-literally-addictive-new-evidence-suggests.

8. "Self-determination theory," Wikimedia Foundation, last modified January 5, 2026, https://en.wikipedia.org/wiki/Self-determination_theory.

9. Sheena S. Iyengar and Mark R. Lepper, "When Choice is Demotivating: Can One Desire Too Much of a Good Thing?" *Journal of Personality and Social Psychology* 79, no. 6 (2000): 995–1006, https://faculty.washington.edu/jdb/345/345%20Articles/Iyengar%20%26%20Lepper%20(2000).pdf.

10. Michael Sailer et al., "How gamification motivates: An experimental study of the effects of specific game design elements on psychological need satisfaction," *Computers in Human Behavior* 69 (April 2016): 371–380, https://www.sciencedirect.com/science/article/pii/S074756321630855X.

11. "Blood Donor Rewards," American Red Cross, accessed January 3, 2025, https://www.redcrossblood.org/donate-blood/blood-donor-rewards.html.

12. Guilia Cambieri, "Loneliness is hurting our health, but these policies could help," Harvard School of Public Health, September 12, 2024, https://hsph.harvard.edu/news/loneliness-is-hurting-our-health-but-these-policies-could-help.

13. Michael Sailer et al., "How gamification motivates: An experimental study of the effects of specific game design elements on psychological need satisfaction."

14. Mei-Lan Lin et al., "The Psychological Motivations to Social Innovation and Transmitting Role of Social Worth."

15. "Expectancy–value theory," Wikimedia, last modified September 8, 2025, https://en.wikipedia.org/wiki/Expectancy-value_theory.

16. Kyle Harrison, "Carbon Offset Demand Hits Record in 2023 Off Huge December," *BloombergNEF,* January 11, 2024, https://about.bnef.com/blog/carbon-offset-demand-hits-record-in-2023-off-huge-december.

17. Daisy Dunne and Yanine Quiroz, "Mapped: The impacts of carbon-offset projects around the world," *Carbon Brief,* September 26, 2023, https://interactive.carbonbrief.org/carbon-offsets-2023/mapped.html.

18. Elizabeth Willmott, "How Microsoft is using an internal carbon fee to reach its carbon negative goal," Microsoft, March 24, 2022, https://www.microsoft.com/en-us/industry/blog/sustainability/2022/03/24/how-microsoft-is-using-an-internal-carbon-fee-to-reach-its-carbon-negative-goal.

19. Brad Smith, "We're increasing our carbon fee as we double down on sustainability," Microsoft, April 15, 2019, https://blogs.microsoft.com/on-the-issues/2019/04/15/were-increasing-our-carbon-fee-as-we-double-down-on-sustainability.

20. Yuzhan Hang et al., "Social expectations as a possible mechanism for adult personality change: Limited empirical evidence for the social investment

principle," *Journal of Personality* 91, no. 6 (December 2023): 1314-1325, https://pubmed.ncbi.nlm.nih.gov/36650725.

21. Alane K. Daugherty, "The Science of Novelty," *Psychology Today*, January 21, 2022, https://www.psychologytoday.com/us/blog/healing-stress-the-inside-out/202201/the-science-novelty.

22. R.M. Emerson, "Social Exchange Theory," *Annual Review of Sociology* 2 (1976): 335–362, https://www.annualreviews.org/content/journals/10.1146/annurev.so.02.080176.002003.

23. "Understand team effectiveness," Google re:Work, accessed January 3, 2025, https://rework.withgoogle.com/en/guides/understanding-team-effectiveness.

24. Jennifer L. Aaker, "Dimensions of Brand Personality," *Journal of Marketing Research* 34, no. 3 (August 1997): 347–356, https://www.jstor.org/stable/3151897.

25. Enrique P. Becerra and Vishag Badrinarayanan, "The influence of brand trust and brand identification on brand evangelism," *Journal of Product & Brand Placement* 22, no. 5-6 (August 19, 2013): 371–383, https://www.emerald.com/insight/content/doi/10.1108/JPBM-09-2013-0394/full/html.

Chapter 7

1. Martin Oscarsson et al., "A large-scale experiment on New Year's resolutions: Approach-oriented goals are more successful than avoidance-oriented goals," *PLOS ONE* 15, no. 12 (December 9, 2020), https://journals.plos.org/plosone/article?id=10.1371/journal.pone.0234097.

2. Petter Johansson et al., "Failure to Detect Mismatches Between Intention and Outcome in a Simple Decision Task," *Science* 310, no. 5745 (October 7, 2005): 116–119, https://www.science.org/doi/10.1126/science.1111709.

3. Philip Parnamets and Jay Van Bavel, "How Political Opinions Change," *Scientific American*, November 20, 2018, https://www.scientificamerican.com/article/how-political-opinions-change.

4. Han Zheng and Rich Ling, "Drivers of social media fatigue: a systematic review," *Telematics and Informatics* 64 (November 2021), https://www.sciencedirect.com/science/article/abs/pii/S0736585321001350.

5. Stacey McLachlan, "The Science of Habit," *Healthline*, December 22, 2021, https://www.healthline.com/health/the-science-of-habit.

6. "Hanns Scharff," Wikimedia Foundation, last modified February 4, 2026, https://en.wikipedia.org/wiki/Hanns_Scharff.

7. Giles Milton, "Secret 'Luxury Prison' Trent Park Helped the Brits Spy on Nazi Generals," *Historynet*, December 17, 2019, https://www.historynet.com/secret-luxury-prison-trent-park-helped-the-brits-spy-on-nazi-generals.

8. "Daryl Davis," Wikimedia Foundation, last modified January 10, 2026, https://en.wikipedia.org/wiki/Daryl_Davis.

9. "Exploring the Brain's Relationship to Habits," U.S. National Science Foundation, January 14, 2013, https://new.nsf.gov/news/exploring-brains-relationship-habits.

10. Christopher Summerfield and Floris P. de Lange, "Expectation in perceptual decision making: neural and computational mechanisms," *Nature Reviews Neuroscience* 15, no. 11 (October 15, 2014): 745–756, https://www.nature.com/articles/nrn3838.

11. "R. Nicholas Carleton, "Fear of the unknown: One fear to rule them all?" *Journal of Anxiety Disorders* 41 (June 2016): 5–21, https://www.sciencedirect.com/science/article/pii/S0887618516300469.

12. "The Top 10 Fears in America 2023," Chapman University - The Voice of Wilkinson, October 20, 2023, https://blogs.chapman.edu/wilkinson/2023/10/20/the-top-10-fears-in-american-2023.

13. Steven Taylor and Gordon J. G. Asmundson, "Negative attitudes about facemasks during the COVID-19 pandemic: The dual importance of perceived ineffectiveness and psychological reactance," *PLOS ONE* 16, no. 2 (February 17, 2021), https://journals.plos.org/plosone/article?id=10.1371/journal.pone.0246317.

14. Lisa Song, "These Household Brands Want to Redefine What Counts as 'Recyclable'," *ProPublica*, September 9, 2024, https://www.propublica.org/article/recycling-recyclable-plastics-consumer-brands-association.

15. Larry M. Bartels, "Messages Received: The Political Impact of Media Exposure," *The American Political Science Review* 87, no. 2 (June 1993): 267–285, https://www.jstor.org/stable/2939040.

16. Tze Wei Liew et al., "Exploring the affective, motivational and cognitive effects of pedagogical agent enthusiasm in a multimedia learning environment," *Human-centric Computing and Information Sciences* 7, no. 9 (May 5, 2017), https://link.springer.com/article/10.1186/s13673-017-0089-2.

17. Lisa Rivero, "Shame and Motivation to Change," *Psychology Today*, January 29, 2015, https://www.psychologytoday.com/us/blog/creative-synthesis/201501/shame-and-motivation-to-change.

18. Brian Lickel et al., "Shame and the motivation to change the self," *Emotion* 14, no. 6 (December 2014): 1049–1061, https://pubmed.ncbi.nlm.nih.gov/25401288.

19. Silvia Grappi et al., "Fashion without pollution: How consumers evaluate brands after an NGO campaign aimed at reducing toxic chemicals in the fashion industry," *Journal of Cleaner Production* 149 (April 15, 2017): 1164–1173, https://www.sciencedirect.com/science/article/abs/pii/S0959652617304092.

20. "Me Too Movement," Wikimedia Foundation, last modified February 2, 2026, https://en.wikipedia.org/wiki/MeToo_movement.

21. Audrey Carlsen et al., "#MeToo Brought Down 201 Powerful Men. Nearly Half of Their Replacements Are Women," *The New York Times,* October 29, 2018, https://www.nytimes.com/interactive/2018/10/23/us/metoo-replacements.html.

22. Simon L. Albrecht et al., "The psychological conditions for employee engagement in organizational change: Test of a change engagement model," *Frontiers in Psychology* 14 (January 20, 2023), https://www.frontiersin.org/journals/psychology/articles/10.3389/fpsyg.2023.1071924/full.

23. Ann M. Graybiel and Kyle S. Smith, "How the Brain Makes and Breaks Habits," *Scientific American*, June 1, 2014, https://www.scientificamerican.com/article/how-the-brain-makes-and-breaks-habits.

24. Wendy Wood and David T. Neal, "Healthy through Habit: Interventions for Initiating & Maintaining Health Behavior Change," *Behavioral Science & Policy* 2, no. 1 (April 1, 2016): 71–83, https://journals.sagepub.com/doi/10.1177/237946151600200109.

25. Martijn van Zomeren et al., "Toward an integrative social identity model of collective action: a quantitative research synthesis of three socio-psychological perspectives," *Psychological Bulletin* 134, no. 4 (July 2008): 504–535, https://pubmed.ncbi.nlm.nih.gov/18605818.

26. Hioko Tabuch and Lisa Freidman, "Oil Executives Grilled Over industry's Role in Climate Disinformation," *The New York Times,* November 9, 2021, https://www.nytimes.com/2021/10/28/climate/oil-executives-house-disinformation-testimony.html.

Chapter 8

1. Michael Barnett and Raymond Duvall, "Power in International Politics," *International Organization* 59, no. 1 (February 15, 2005), https://www.cambridge.org/core/journals/international-organization/article/power-in-international-politics/F5F3C74D30A12A5C4CC9B4EFEA152967.

2. Flor Avelino, "Theories of power and social change. Power contestations and their implications for research on social change and innovation," *Journal of Political Power* 14, no. 3 (March 7, 2021): 425–448, https://www.tandfonline.com/doi/full/10.1080/2158379X.2021.1875307#abstract.

3. Rebecca Doherty et al., "The triple play: Growth, profit, and sustainability," McKinsey & Company, August 9, 2023, https://www.mckinsey.com/capabilities/strategy-and-corporate-finance/our-insights/the-triple-play-growth-profit-and-sustainability.

4. "National Health Expenditure Data," Centers for Medicare & Medicaid Services, last modified January 14, 2026, https://www.cms.gov/data-research/statistics-trends-and-reports/national-health-expenditure-data/historical.

5. Hamza Shad, "VC funding in healthcare has been more resilient than other industries," Carta, June 6, 2024, https://carta.com/data/health-tech-2024.

6. "The Ultimate List of Charitable Giving Statistics for 2024," Nonprofits Source, accessed January 3, 2025, https://nonprofitssource.com/online-giving-statistics.

7. Eliana Zeballos et al., "A Disaggregated View of Market Concentration in the Food Retail Industry," U.S. Department of Agriculture *Economic Research Report Number 314* (January 5, 2023), https://www.ers.usda.gov/publications/pub-details?pubid=105557.

8. "U.S. Food System Factsheet," University of Michigan Center for Sustainable Systems, accessed January 3, 2025, https://css.umich.edu/publications/factsheets/food/us-food-system-factsheet.

9. James M. MacDonald, "Concentration in U.S. Meatpacking Industry and How It Affects Competition and Cattle Prices," *Amber Waves*, January 25, 2024, https://www.ers.usda.gov/amber-waves/2024/january/concentration-in-u-s-meatpacking-industry-and-how-it-affects-competition-and-cattle-prices.

10. Caroline O'Donovan, "Fighting back against data centers, one small town at a time," *The Washington Post*, October 5, 2024, https://www.washingtonpost.com/technology/2024/10/05/data-center-protest-community-resistance.

11. Kat So, "Climate Deniers of the 118th Congress," Center for American Progress, July 18, 2024, https://www.americanprogress.org/article/climate-deniers-of-the-118th-congress.

12. Robert J. Brulle, "Institutionalizing delay: foundation funding and the creation of U.S. climate change counter-movement organizations," *Climatic Change* 122 (December 21, 2013): 681–694, https://link.springer.com/article/10.1007/s10584-013-1018-7.

13. Justin Farrell, "Corporate funding and ideological polarization about climate change," *Proceedings of the National Academy of Sciences of the United States* 113, no. 1 (November 23, 2015): 92–97, https://www.pnas.org/doi/full/10.1073/pnas.1509433112

14. "Business and Industry Time Series/Trend Charts," U.S. Census Bureau, last modified February 11, 2026, https://www.census.gov/econ/currentdata/?programCode=BFS&startYear=2004&endYear=2024&categories[]=TOTAL&dataType=BA_BA&geoLevel=US&adjusted=1&notAdjusted=1&errorData=0#table-results

15. Lanre Dahunsi, "The Emotional Cycle of Change – Navigating the Valley of Despair," Lanredahunsi.com, June 22, 2021, https://www.lanredahunsi.com/the-emotional-cycle-of-change-navigating-the-valley-of-despair.

Acknowledgments

I'd like to thank Hilary Claggett at Georgetown University Press, without whom this book would still be just an idea, along with Susan Shankin and the team at Precocity Press for their help elevating and presenting the content.

Dave Feldman at Bethesda Green and Jonathan Graham at the Sustainable Green Printing Partnership have provided invaluable input on the practical challenges of sustainable businesses over the years.

The team at Young Marketing Consulting, particularly Ben Huizinga and Alison Napolitano, has given me the time and headspace to dedicate to this project.

And finally my wife Wendy and son Noah, for putting up with evening and weekend writing sessions amidst our hectic lives.

About the Author

TIM YOUNG is an entrepreneur, advocate, and growth strategist dedicated to helping organizations turn purpose into measurable impact. For more than 25 years, he has helped organizations—from early-stage startups to Fortune 500 companies—build marketing strategies that drive real impact, including mission-driven nonprofits and cause-based initiatives.

He began his career advising global brands like Target, Sony, and Kimberly-Clark during the early evolution of digital marketing, and went on to lead marketing for the international nonprofit Entrepreneurs' Organization, where he helped double its global membership and launch initiatives such as the Global Student Entrepreneur Awards.

In 2013, Tim founded Young Marketing Consulting, which has since grown into a full-service agency specializing in growth strategy, differentiation, and high-impact marketing execution. His work focuses on helping organizations compete more effectively—especially those working to create meaningful social and economic change.

Tim is also president of the Washington Network Group and lives just outside Washington, DC.

For more information, visit youngmarketingconsulting.com.

Made in the USA
Monee, IL
08 November 2026

68007850R00114